Dedication

This book is dedicated to the memory of Edgar C. "Eddie" Register, a Fort Pierce native who died Nov. 12, 2010, at the age of 93. A World War II veteran and retired banker and Chamber of Commerce executive, Mr. Register was devoted to his family and community. He was a class act, always considerate and a true Southern gentleman. He had a keen interest in history throughout his life. In fact, he was looking forward to speaking on a veterans' panel at Indian River State College last fall when his final illness struck. Mr. Register loved to tell stories about early Fort Pierce for the WQCS oral history project. His tales about storms, war and everyday life always made for good radio. He is greatly missed.

Edgar C. "Eddie" Register and Janie Gould at WQCS in September 2010

Introduction

Volume II of "Floridays: Stories from Under the Sun," is a continuation of my radio interviews, in print form, about interesting, unusual or otherwise noteworthy people and places in Florida. The stories included here were heard first on WQCS 88.9 FM. Most have also been aired on the statewide radio newsmagazine, "Florida Frontiers," produced by the Florida Historical Society.

The popular "Floridays" radio series began as an oral history project for WQCS. I interviewed more than 300 people about local history, and produced shows on Florida during the Depression, war and hurricanes, among many other topics. Later, the project evolved into radio features on off beat topics and notable personal experiences. In this volume, you'll read about a man who swam in the "Creature from the Black Lagoon" films; a couple that used to capture "nuisance alligators;" a long-gone sugar mill; a kerosene-based home remedy for cuts and burns, and much, much more. I hope these stories will make you smile or say to yourself, "I never knew that!"

You received this book as our way of thanking you for your generous membership contribution to WQCS. We are increasingly dependent on listener support to maintain the quality programming that you expect. Enjoy this book, and please tell your friends about it! And please continue to listen to WQCS wherever you are and in whatever manner you choose - on your radio, computer or smart phone.

Thank you for your support.

Janie Gould
WQCS 88.9 FM
September 2011

Floridays

Volume II

Stories From Under the Sun

ISBN: 1466214597
EAN-13:9781466214590

Production and design: Michele Calvo
Cover: Antonio Velarde

WQCS 88.9 FM
3209 Virginia Avenue
Fort Pierce, FL 34981

Floridays: Listen Fridays at 7:20a.m. or 6 p.m. on 88.9 FM or at wqcs.org. Hear past **Floridays** shows by going to wqcs.org. Click on Programming and then Audio Archive. If you have an idea for a Floridays story, please contact Janie Gould at 772-462-7822 or send an email to her at Jgould@irsc.edu.

HOW TO ORDER THIS BOOK
"Floridays: Tales from Under the Sun, Volume II," is a gift exclusively for WQCS members who donate $150 or more to the station annually. To make your donation, please make your check payable to WQCS 88.9 FM and mail it to the address listed above. To pay by credit card, call 772-462-7813 or make your donation online at www.wqcs.org.

On the Cover: If it's true, as the saying goes, that "red sky at night, sailor's delight," then mariners must have had some smooth sailing after this sunset at the Adams Ranch west of Fort Pierce. (Photo by Bud Adams)

Contents

Contents

Politics,
The Environment
and Race

Section 1

William Jennings Bryan with his brother, Charles, at Bryan's home in Miami (Florida Archives)

'Great Commoner' Bryan Became Florida Booster

*W*illiam Jennings Bryan, the Gilded Age populist known as the Great Commoner, ran for president three times and served as U.S. secretary of state. Then he was a major player in the "Monkey Trial" that challenged the teaching of evolution in Tennessee. Like so many other people, he spent his twilight years in Florida, but he was anything but retired. Michael Blayney, a retired history professor from Bryan's home state of Nebraska, has studied Bryan's time in Florida during the Roaring Twenties. Bryan was known as a great orator and in Florida used his speaking talents to promote Miami real estate, which made him rich. But Blayney says money was not his sole motivation.

"He really believed in Florida. He believed in the future of Florida, that someday Florida would be part of a greater Pan-American civilization. He had two introductions to Florida when he was younger. The first one was when his fiancée took a winter vacation to Florida with his parents, and she wrote him about the orange groves and orange blossoms, and Florida was kind of an idyllic subtropical paradise. That was his first image of Florida."

Q:"His first unseen image of Florida!"

A: "Unseen! But then, during the Spanish-American War he had a regiment, the Nebraska Regiment. They camped in a place they called Cuba Libre, which was outside Jacksonville. There he suffered heat, humidity, snakes. Dozens of men came down with malaria and typhoid. He came down with a case of typhoid fever. Finally, he wrote his wife and said please come down and take care of me, which she did. He never saw action in the Spanish-American War."

Q: "He never went to Cuba?"

A: "No. He never went to Cuba, and that was his first actual experience with Florida."

Q: "An ignominious beginning to his Florida years?"

A: "Yes. Exactly."

Q: "But he gave the state another chance?"

A: "Yes, he did, because of his wife. She suffered from arthritis. The climate was good for her."

Q: "Now, Bryan's real estate work in Florida is well known, but he was also involved in Florida politics. I guess he couldn't stay out of politics!"

A: "No, he couldn't. First of all, he tried to influence the Florida Legislature to outlaw the teaching of evolution in the public schools."

Q: "Was he successful in that regard?"

A: "No. The controversy centered around the image of Florida. They weren't concerned about evolution itself so much as an issue as they were that it wouldn't do the state any good; it wouldn't attract Northerners to come down to Florida."

Q: "It wouldn't make the state seem progressive?"

A: "Progressive in the eyes of the North."

Q: "He also tried to promote, you were telling me, a favorite son of Florida, the president of the University of Florida, A.A. Murphree, as president of the United States."

A: "He was a friend of Bryan. Bryan put forth his name at the Democratic convention in 1924."

Q: "Did he think that Murphree had a chance of being elected?"

A: "No, but Bryan thought that this would be a symbol for Florida, showing that he was serious about having roots in Florida."

Q: "What was Bryan's legacy for Florida?"

A: "He wanted Florida, first of all, to be a real civilization with roots, not just as the essayist Philip Wylie later said, a tropical Coney Island where people would come down to resorts but wouldn't have real roots in Florida. The other thing that he wanted was for Florida to be a middle-class civilization, not just for extremely wealthy people. He was progressive, ahead of his time on all issues with the exception of race. He was really a racist, a segregationist. He didn't say much about race in his campaigns. He emphasized it when he moved down to Florida."

Blayney discussed Bryan's Florida years as part of the WQCS Speakers Series in 2010. Blayney spoke at the Heritage Center in downtown Vero Beach, not far from the site where Bryan himself orated in 1925. A marker outside the Heritage Center commemorates Bryan's local appearance.

Sen. Matthew Quay in Indian headdress
(Provided by Jean Ellen Wilson)

Northern Political Boss Put St. Lucie on the Map

*D*uring the late 19th century, a well-connected political boss from Philadelphia named Matthew Quay discovered the Indian River. He built a home in St. Lucie, now known as St. Lucie Village, and spent more than a dozen winters enjoying the tarpon fishing and mild weather. Quay was a powerful member of the U.S. Senate and a Republican kingmaker. His enemies branded him a drunk and thief, and after he died in 1904 he was pretty much forgotten. St. Lucie County native Jean-Ellen Wilson had never even heard of Quay when she was growing up many years later. Then, while she was working in Washington, D.C., she came across Quay's name and a link to St. Lucie and found that his Florida papers were in the Library of Congress. In his papers she found newspaper interviews with him that were datelined St. Lucie, from 1890.

"At that time, coming to St. Lucie would be like going to Africa now on safari. There were no roads. The railroad wasn't here yet. There were something like four families between Vero and Jupiter."

Q: "Theodore Roosevelt knew him and liked him …"

A: "Yes."

Q: "Did you ever find any record of (Roosevelt) coming here?"

A: "No, but I have a copy of a telegram he sent to Senator Quay at St. Lucie. Quay called his house Kill-Care. 'To Matthew at Kill-Care. I have done what you asked me to do.'"

Q: "And you don't know what that was?"

A: No."

Q: "Made Grand Canyon a national park, possibly?"

A: "Maybe gave some postmaster a job, who knows!"

Q: "Probably something like that. Quay, if he's known at all, is known for getting funds to dredge the Intracoastal, but you say he did a lot more."

A: "Any bill that was in the coffers in Congress that was going to aid South Florida, he would get behind. At that time we did not have particularly influential senators, so he would be the lead senator."

Q: "Quay's public image was sometimes less than stellar."

A: "Oh yes."

Q: "Why was that?"

A: "Well, he was very shrewd. He could be ruthless, and he wanted to win in politics. So he made enemies. But I'm so bookish that I have to say that somebody who reads a lot can't be all bad. He had one of the finest libraries in the United States. He had a cousin who he got elected governor of Pennsylvania. They exchanged letters in Latin! He was a learned, thoughtful man. He gave money to all kinds of local causes. He put the place on the map so other wealthy people started coming."

Q: "He had a niece who came down…"

A: "Her name was Marian Quay. There was a house party in the Quay compound and one morning she thought she'd go fishing, but then one of the Summerlins, I think it was Clarence, said it was a good day for a gator hunt. So Clarence and Aden took her and her cousin on a gator hunt. They made noises at this gator pond to try to bring out this gator. They 'grumbled it up.'"

Q: "You mean the gator sound?"

A: "Yes. Well, finally the gator came up and she shot it. Well, it turned out to be, I think she said, an 'ignominious three feet,' and her cousin could not stop laughing. She said you shot that gator in your gloves and veil! The members of the house party laughed at her so much about this little tiny gator that she decided she was going to go back out there. This time they have a pole with a hook on it that they keep sticking in the bottom of the pond until they hit a gator. The gator jumped up and she shot it right between the eyes! She took the skin back up north to Philadelphia."

Q: "A true Florida souvenir!'

Jean- Ellen Wilson regrets that there are few local reminders of Matthew Quay.

A: "There's one little alley or back street in St. Lucie Village called Quay Way. This guy knew every important person in the United States and he was here almost every year from 1885 until his death in 1904."

There's also a Quay Dock Road in Indian River County. The community of Winter Beach used to be called Quay, but the name was changed during the land boom of the 1920s.

*Former Okeechobee County Sheriff "Pogy Bill" Collins
(Courtesy of Dan Thomas)*

Colorful Okeechobee Sheriff Memorialized in Song

O ne of the most interesting characters in Okeechobee's history was a hard- drinking fisherman named William Collins. Everyone called him Pogy Bill, because he tried to pass off some baitfish, known as pogies, as catfish. Pogy Bill was appointed town marshal while serving a jail term. Later, he was elected sheriff. It was around 1915, when Okeechobee was still a frontier. Erich Overhultz, a lieutenant in the Broward Sheriff's Office, is also a musician and Florida history buff who has studied the life of Pogy Bill.

"He had a penchant for getting drunk and getting into brawls."

Q: "Sheriff Pogy Bill did a little moonshine on the side, right?"

A: "He wasn't so much a moonshiner himself, but he allowed it to happen, kind of looked the other way. He kind of had a dim view of Prohibition. Even though he had quit drinking he felt that as long as a person could control himself he didn't see any problem with a person having a drink every now and then."

Q:"Was moonshine a big business in Okeechobee?"

A: "Absolutely. It became even more important when the hurricanes hit, the '26 one and especially the '28 one. They really devastated the fishing industry and wrecked a lot of towns around the lake. Moonshine became a very viable source of hard cash. Pogy saw it as a necessary evil. He didn't like the feds sticking their nose in things."

Q: "The revenooers!"

A: "Right! It was reported that Al Capone's people had approached him about making inroads into the lake territory because they were already operating in Dade and Broward counties. He told them in no uncertain terms that they were not welcome, and they backed off. He could be a tough character!"

Q: "He did some jail time himself ..."

A: "Yes. Not for the moonshine which he was later convicted of, but prior to being appointed the town marshal he did 90 days in jail. It was a situation when Judge Hancock had sent a deputy to talk to Pogy about his hell-raising ways. On Saturday nights, the town was known for fishermen and cowboys and sawmill workers getting into fights. They would literally tear up the town. Businesses would be ransacked. One person even reported seeing three different fights happening at the same time, one inside a bar, one outside the bar, and one out on the street. What happened was when the deputy went to talk to Pogy, some of Pogy's friends intercepted the guy and actually disarmed him and then tossed the deputy into a muddy creek. Pogy actually declared himself judge. He held court in a grocery store while barefoot. He declared each of his friends guilty and he fined them a quart of whiskey apiece, which they all polished off. Pogy thought it was just a big joke and was having fun with it, but Judge Hancock wasn't too amused. He had Pogy arrested."

Q: "So when Pogy was in jail, he was named town marshal. How did that happen?"

A: "Some of the town's leading citizens were desperate to have someone that could come in and really lay down the law in the town. The town was growing, but at the same time they needed some control there. They knew that deep down inside, Pogy was basically a good guy. He had a unique system of justice. Any time he and his buddies would tear up the town, if there were any innocent bystanders he would make sure they were compensated. So they came to Judge Hancock with a proposal. If Pogy would behave himself, please let him out and appoint him as town marshal. Pogy agreed to the deal. By all accounts he really cleaned up the town. He arrested a lot of the people who he actually had torn up the town with."

Q: "Some of his old buddies?"

A: "Yes. His old buddies."

While serving as sheriff, Pogy Bill was charged in a moonshine conspiracy.

"He tried to run again while the case was on appeal. He lost by three votes".

A restaurant in Okeechobee is named for Pogy Bill, and Erich Overhultz recently recorded a song about the legendary lawman.

Scene in Florida's Everglades (Florida Archives)

1911 Report Reveals Mind-Set About Everglades

*V*al Martin sits surrounded by a happy clutter of Floridiana in his publishing house and bookstore in Hobe Sound. He deals in Florida books and maps. He reprints classics such as "Jonathan Dickinson's Journal," the story of a shipwreck off Jupiter Inlet that was first published in 1699. He published the 50th anniversary paperback edition of

Marjory Stoneman Douglas' influential book about the Everglades, "River of Grass." He's done Theodore Pratt's historical novel, "The Barefoot Mailman," which became a movie, and numerous other tomes about treasure, nature and history. My first question, I thought, was an obvious one.

Q: "If you had to pick your favorite book about Florida, what would it be?"

A: "Senate Document Number 89, printed by the 62nd Congress in 1911."

Q: "It's a report about the Everglades written way before anybody thought about saving it. You republished it with a new cover and you're calling it, 'A Study in Bureaucratic Self-Deception: South Florida in Peril.' So tell me, what did the Senate conclude in 1911 about the Everglades?"

A: "They concluded that draining the Everglades was a do-able project."

Q: "What did this report do? Did it founder on a shelf somewhere in Washington for a long time? How did you get a hold of it?"

A: "I ran across a copy of it in an unbound edition in a book store in Pensacola, when I was out traveling around the state opening retail book accounts. It sat on my shelf for 15 or 20 years until all the activity began around the early 1990s for restoring the Everglades. I pulled it off the shelf and reprinted it."

Q: "Had you read it thoroughly until that time?"

A: "No. I began reading it in the mid-1990s, and I read it twice. It was so fascinating, so full of documentation from very early surveys."

Q: "So really, it gives a framework for what they were planning to do. It doesn't say it was good or bad. It just lays out the parameters for how they were going to drain this swamp."

A: "Exactly right."

Q: "So this book was on a shelf somewhere in Pensacola. It probably hadn't been opened since 1911, and you brought it back and republished it.

A: "And believe it or not, it's a very poor seller. Marjory Douglas' book is far and away the most popular book on the history of the Everglades."

Q: "Do you think the government jargon is just a little bit too dry for the average reader?"

A: "That might be a possibility, but for anybody who is interested in the subject of the drainage of the Everglades, I believe this report is the benchmark reference."

Q: "Are you always on the lookout for something like this in your travels around Florida?"

A: "Absolutely!"

Q: Are you looking for anything specific right now?"

A: "No, but I haven't been doing much traveling either. I'm pretty much focused on distributing what I've already published."

Q: "Tell me about your own book reading."

A: "I like to read a lot of current nonfiction that has to do with the subject of where we are today in America. I just finished Jesse Ventura's book, 'American Conspiracies.' "

Q: "Have you read most of the major Florida authors?"

A: "I can't say that I have. There are so many good ones. I've read maybe a dozen."

Q: "A hundred years from now, which Florida authors are still going to be read?"

A: "Marjory Douglas, Patrick Smith, Theodore Pratt."

Q: "If you were going to be a on a desert island and could take only one book, what would it be?"

A: "'Jonathan Dickinson's Journal.'"

Q: "What's its appeal?"

A: "The realization of what the survivors from the wreck of the Reformation had to go through in order to escape captivity in southern Florida at the hands of the Indians, and walk the beach from Jupiter Inlet to St. Augustine."

Q: "It's incredible that any of them survived!"

A: "Absolutely. All you have to do is try to put yourself in their shoes. It's a mind-boggling experience."

Q: "And they didn't even have shoes!"

A: "You're correct. They didn't have shoes or clothes!"

Val Martin owns Florida Classics Library in Hobe Sound.

The John Scott Healing Garden is on the main campus of Martin Memorial Health Systems in Stuart. (Provided by Martin Memorial Health Systems)

Man Saw Racial Customs Change at Stuart's Hospital

*J*ohn Scott was young in 1939 and Martin County Hospital was new when the administrator offered him a job as a gardener for $30 a month. He accepted, and when the only orderly in the hospital quit, he got his job. He soon learned how to prepare patients for surgery and assist during operations, which mostly involved repairing hernias or removing appendixes. He was single at the time --- he didn't meet his wife, Bertha, until later -- so he lived in a room in the hospital basement.

"I was on call 24 hours a day!"

Jupiter Island philanthropists William and Francoise Barstow had paid for construction of the hospital. They stipulated that its doors must be open to all, without racial discrimination. Inside the hospital, patients in the early years were segregated by race.

"They had whites on one side and blacks on the other side," said Scott, who is black. Now on the other end they had a colored nursery and a white nursery."

The operating room was often sweltering, since nothing was air conditioned.

"We had two big fans out in the hallway."

Q: "Did that help?"

A: "No! We didn't feel that in there."

The surgeons worked under intense lights that made it even hotter. One doctor asked Scott to help him with a problem, but he didn't call him by his name.

"He said, Willie, wipe the sweat off my face."

Q: "Why didn't he call you John?"

A: "Well, he just liked Willie the best. The lady who was giving the anesthesia, she picked up on that. She said, Doctor, his name ain't Willie. It's John. He said, well, I just like Willie the best."

Racial customs at the hospital started changing during World War II. Two GIs who were buddies were admitted.

"One was white and the other one was black, and somehow or other we made a mistake and put both of them in the same room."

A nurse told the soldiers they'd have to be separated, but they refused, Scott said.

"They said we're in the Army together and we're going to stay here together!"

A few years after the war, a hurricane blew through and left Scott with some more lasting memories.

"It was so bad water was rushing down the hallway and we had to move all the machines out of the operating room."

Besides working as an orderly, Scott earned certification as a licensed practical nurse. He helped the late Dr. Julian Parker deliver babies, too. Parker delivered 4,000 babies during his career, including 31 sets of twins. Scott also worked in the X-ray department and in medical records.

Q: "You never missed a day of work in 68 years?"

A: "Oh, I bumped my leg and had to leave for a few weeks."

Q: "And that was the only time?"

A: "Yeah."

Q: "Could I ask you how old you are?"

A:"I thought you'd get around to that. I was born Sept. 8, 1915, and I feel like I'm 45."

Q: "What do you attribute your long and healthy life to?"

A: "Well, I just take care of myself. I go to bed when it's time to go to bed, and I go to church, and I read my Bible and I come to work and do my job."

Scott's mother gave him some advice a long time ago that served him well over the years: "Mind your own business, hear and don't hear, see and don't see."

Martin Memorial Health Systems dedicated its John Scott Healing Garden to the longtime employee, who retired several years ago.

President Truman had strong ties to Florida. Here, he waves to people in Key West after his 1948 election victory. (Florida Archives)

After Truman's Yacht Ran Aground, Congress Acted

*P*resident Truman was inconvenienced once in Vero Beach and the results were far reaching. William Crawford, author of a book about Florida's Intracoastal Waterway, says Congress decided to widen and deepen the waterway in 1945.

"Unfortunately, Congress didn't authorize the spending of any money; 1945 came and went, 1946 came and went, 1947, '48, '49, and then in the spring of 1950 two things happened. President Harry Truman was cruising down the Intracoastal Waterway in his presidential yacht. The former secretary of the Navy, Jon L. Sullivan, was also traveling (separately). According to the mayor of Vero Beach, Alex MacWilliam, both yachts were grounded in the Vero Beach area. As a result, Congress got into action and in 1950 passed the necessary funding to increase the depth."

30

Q: "Was this the presidential yacht, the Sequoia?"

A: "Can't tell. There were several. In all likelihood it was the Sequoia."

Q: "Where was Truman going?"

A: "Probably down to Key West."

Q: "Had he been opposed to spending money for dredging up to that point?"

A: "Yes, and even Congress, the majority of Congress, was opposed. This was a long-standing issue, whether or not Congress should be responsible for dredging and maintaining the inland waterways, or whether the state and local entities should be in charge of funding."

Q: "So Truman thought that federal funds should not be used for that until his own presidential yacht ran aground?"

A: "He was against the funding. It was not a high priority for him."

Q: "How did he react? What do your records tell you?"

A: "The records don't say, except that soon afterwards, Congress finally approved the deepening of the waterway. Eventually, by 1960, the waterway was 12 feet deep all the way to Fort Pierce."

Q: "And that allowed for boats of what size?"

A: "Large yacht size and maybe some barge traffic, but not very large boats. At the time, boats were not nearly the size they are today."

Q: "The channel was deepened eventually to 12 feet?"

A: "That's sometimes referred to as the controlling depth. It's supposed to be 12 feet today. But a lot of mariners will tell you in many stretches of the waterway it's not 12 feet. For at least a decade Congress has seriously neglected the funding of the Intracoastal Waterway."

Q: "So it's still happening?"

A: "It's still happening. Fortunately, we have some stimulus money, which is making up for a number of years of neglect."

Q: "Let's go back to Truman for a minute. How long was he delayed in the Vero Beach area?"

A: "He was delayed a few hours."

Q: "Did he leave the boat?"

A: "No."

Q: "But he was impatient and a little bit upset?"

A: "He was delayed and this was very common. In the early years there were a lot of groundings because the waterway was not deep enough and it wasn't well maintained."

Q: "Do you think it was a good object lesson for the president?"

A: "Exactly. The kind of things that Truman experienced are happening now on the Intracoastal Waterway in Georgia and South Carolina, where people get stuck all the time."

Q: "So it's a constant battle to keep it navigable?"

A: "A constant battle!"

Q: "If Truman's yacht hadn't run aground when it did, what do you think would have happened?"

A: "There probably wouldn't have been any funding, because there was a big fight at that time. It's a fight that goes all the way back to the founding of the nation, when people in Congress felt that the inland waterways were local and state problems, not federal problems."

Q: "Did Truman come this way again?"

A: "I'm sure he did."

Q: "And as far as you know, his ship never ran aground again?"

A: "Not again."

Q: "Once was enough to get Congress moving. Right?

A: "Right!"

William Crawford is the author of "Florida's Big Dig: the Atlantic Intracoastal Waterway." He practices law in Broward County.

President Truman shakes hands with Key West police officers before departing from the island. (Florida Archives)

An elementary school in Fort Pierce is named for a teacher who was forced out of St. Lucie County schools decades ago. (Photo by Janie Gould)

Black Educator Banished from St. Lucie County Schools

*T*he first black judge in St. Lucie County, Ralph Flowers, came to Fort Pierce in 1959 to become the band director at Lincoln Park High School. He was in the Army at the time and drove down from Fort Knox, Ky., to interview with the school principal, Leroy Floyd.

"I came down Avenue D, I guess, and I had to come down some dirt roads and I'm in my brand new car!   It was a Fairlane 500, a Ford. That was a horrendous trip. When I arrived at Mr. Floyd's house, you couldn't tell that I even owned a car."

Q: "Pretty muddy, I guess? It had been raining and the roads were all dirt."

A: "That's absolutely right. When I was traveling on the dirt roads I said I don't know what I got myself into here and I'm only going to stay one year.

I lived with C.A. Moore, Chester A. Moore, on the corner of 13th Street and Avenue D."

Q: "He was a generation ahead of you. He taught here at one time and then you were telling me something happened…"

A: "From what I understand, he was somewhat blackballed here because of his political ideas. He was able to get a job up in Indian River County, to which he rode a bike every morning to and from."

Q: "That would have been to Gifford. Right?"

A: "Yes. Gifford High School."

Q: "You said he got involved in political activities in St. Lucie County."

A: "I think it was over registering black people to vote. It was not fashionable during that time for that to happen."

Q: "He rode his bike 20 miles each way?"

A: "It would rain and he had to walk his bike sometimes. He had to get up at three or four o'clock in the morning to get to school on time. He said he was possibly one of the first ones to reach the school."

Q: "Even though he came from the farthest! Did he ever work in St. Lucie County again?"

A: "No, he never did. When I arrived here, he had retired."

Much later, the school board named a new elementary school in Fort Pierce after Moore. Flowers later decided to go to law school.

A: "I always wanted to be a band director and I wanted to learn to fly a plane and I wanted to be a lawyer. I was able to get to Florida A&M to go to law school."

He had roots in St. Lucie County by this time, so after graduating from law school he came back and started practicing law in Fort Pierce. His second case was the landmark legal battle to desegregate St. Lucie County schools, and his first case made headlines around the world. A 20-year-old Army private from Fort Pierce named Pondexteur Williams was killed in Vietnam in 1970. He was black and was refused burial in a white cemetery. Ultimately, a federal judge ordered that he be buried at Hillcrest Memorial Gardens."

"It was a very tense period of time. All the news was focused on Fort Pierce and why they would not let this soldier who gave his life for freedom be buried in the cemetery here."

Q: "When you came here it was a time of complete segregation. It was 1959."

A: "I remember having to go to the back door upstairs at the theatre, which I never did, and I recall having to go to some of the back holes in the restaurants."

Q: "Back holes?"

A: "They had a window that black people had to go to. I remember seeing them going there but I never did. I had been in the service, which was totally desegregated, and I did not believe that I had to spend my money to be degraded like that."

Q: "What's the highlight of your career?

A: "Getting Pondexteur Williams buried was number one. Getting the school system desegregated without a lot of problems was number two, and I guess being accepted by the legal community. They treated me quite well."

Q: "You mentioned that you had always wanted to be a band director, and always wanted to be a lawyer, and always wanted to fly a plane. Did you ever fly a plane?"

A: "When I went to the Army, I applied to the flight school and I was accepted. I've been able to accomplish all of those."

Ralph Flowers is retired and lives in Port St. Lucie.

Gov.-Elect Dan McCarty, right, and Gov. Millard Caldwell ride to inauguration ceremonies in Tallahassee. (Florida Archives)

Former Governor Called 'Forgotten Reformer'

*F*ort Pierce native son Dan McCarty made political history when he was elected governor in 1952. North Florida politicians dominated the state at that time. But McCarty had one of the briefest tenures on record, dying from a heart attack in 1953 at the age of 41. He had been a rancher and citrus grower in St. Lucie County and was a highly decorated veteran of World War II. He served in the Legislature before the war and ran for governor the first time in 1948. Historian, author and Fort Pierce native Robert Taylor has written about McCarty.

Q: "Wasn't he the first governor from South Florida, peninsular Florida?"

A: "He certainly was the first governor from southeastern Florida."

Q: "How was he able to overcome the strength of North Florida?"

A: "Well, Dan McCarty was a person who had made a tremendous impression on his peers during his service in the Legislature. He was a very likeable man; some said a charismatic man, someone who people believed to have integrity, someone who folks would like to follow."

Q: "You call him the forgotten reformer. How come?"

A: "Dan McCarty's career was cut short by his untimely death, and people tend to just sort of dismiss his governorship as not being important, but I see him as part of the World War II generation -- the greatest generation, if you will -- who came home and was dissatisfied with the status quo in his home state."

Q: "With business as it had always been run?"

A: "Yes. Business as usual, with its negative connotations, was something he found unacceptable. He ran as a reformer, as someone who was not part of the good ol' boy political system."

Q: "What, in his short time in office, was he able to do, or start to do?"

A: "Well, he proposed to put how the state operated on a more business- like model. He was a businessman. He had to make payrolls. He had to balance the books at the end of the month. He wanted Florida to do that. He wanted central accounting. He wanted an expanded auditing system. He wanted the state to have an emergency fund."

Q: "There was nothing like that at the time?"

A: "No. Not the size and scope that he wanted."

Q: "He must have met quite a bit of opposition in Tallahassee."

A: "He certainly had some run-ins with the political establishment. Reformers usually do. He made it very clear right from his inaugural address that he planned to change the way business was done in Tallahassee."

Cabinet members and Supreme Court justices at McCarty's burial in St. Lucie County (Florida Archives)

Q: "So what do you think he might have been able to accomplish if he had been able to serve a full term?"

A: "Well, one of the things you learn if you study the brief McCarty era is the man's vision. He was a conservationist, an environmentalist, before it was fashionable."

Q: "That was way ahead of its time!"

A: "Yes. He strongly opposed an idea to drill for oil in Everglades National Park. He wanted to reorganize the various state wildlife and natural resource agencies to make them more efficient. One of the things that struck me was that he was very interested in the potential of television. He wanted very much to have a Florida public television network for the public good and was corresponding with New York Gov. Thomas E. Dewey to see how New York had set up such a system."

Q: "That was when television was in its infancy."

A: "In its early days! Dan McCarty saw that there was something there that Floridians could benefit from.

Q: "You mentioned that there was a plan, or at least a proposal, to drill for oil in the Everglades. Who wanted to do that?"

A: "Private industry."

Q: "How far did they get?"

A: "Not very far. The governor said absolutely not, and Floridians agreed with him."

Q: "Where would he rank, do you think, with 20th century governors?"

A: "Well, I would give him fairly high marks, because most of his reform agenda would later be picked up (by subsequent governors)."

State Rep. Bill Scott, right, with Gov. Farris Bryant, center, Ralph Evinrude and Frances Langford around 1960 in Tallahassee. (Florida Archives)

Pork Chop Gang Used to Dominate Florida Politics

*B*ill Scott was a legislator from Martin County in the late 1950s and early '60s. In those days the Legislature met every other year, and virtually every member of the House and the Senate was white, male and a Democrat. It was a heady time for small counties, such as Martin, St. Lucie and Indian River, because each of Florida's 67 counties had at least one state representative. It was also the height of the Baby Boom. Scott and his wife, Catherine, had a growing family when he was elected to his first term.

Q: "Did you move your family up to Tallahassee each year for the session?"

41

A: "The first term, we had four children and they all had measles -- or chicken pox, one of the two -- just before the session opened. I did not take them with me the first term. We had five children by the time of the second term. We had a prayer breakfast (in Tallahassee) and one of the guys said they used to say the Legislature was inactive between sessions, but the number of babies that had arrived showed we were not as inactive as they thought!"

Q: "The pay for legislators was nothing to write home about."

A: "You received $100 a month except when the Legislature was in session, when I think we got an additional $20 a day. We might have been able to get some postage during the session and during the session they would print our letterhead for us. Legislators had an office in an annex behind the capitol. The office consisted of three or four desks located inside a rather large size room, and a chair or two you could sit in, but that was it. We drew our own bills, although we had a bill drafting assistant. We would get the outline of it and take it down to the bill drafting department."

After the first session, Scott came home from Tallahassee on the train.

A: "When I got to Stuart, they had a welcoming committee there for me!"

There at the railroad station was a cheering crowd consisting of Catherine Scott and the couple's children, waving a banner saying "Welcome Home, Daddy! The rest of the people couldn't have cared less!"

Q: "Was there any business to take care of when the Legislature wasn't in session? You didn't have a local office, a legislative office, did you?"

A: "No. If they wanted me, they called me up, or came over to see me, or got me at lunch time. At that time in the Legislature, you had 120 representatives, of which three – count 'em, one, two, three – were Republicans, all from Pinellas County. In those days, the old folks from up North, if they were Republicans, came down and couldn't do anything but register Republican. They had three representatives and, I believe, one senator. Everybody else was a Democrat."

Q: "Let me ask you this: were you a member of the Pork Chop Gang?"

A: "I sure was."

Q: "And proud of it?"

A: "And proud of it!"

Q: "Even though you were really from South Florida, but a rural county?"

A: "A rural county and South Florida. That's right."

Q: "There might be some people out there who don't know what the Pork Chop Gang was!"

A: "They probably would call it a caucus. Because of our numbers, we could pretty well run the Legislature. There was no national thing that came down to us from a bunch of, excuse the term, yankees."

Q: "Do you know where the term Pork Chop Gang came from?"

A: "It came from eating pork! Pork is a so-called he-man dish. But the lambs, the poor little lambs who lost their way ..."

Q: "In other words, the South Florida urban people were known as the Lambchoppers?"

A: "Well, not only South Florida, because you had Tampa and you had Jacksonville, and you had some leaning towards it out in Pensacola."

Q: "So you were a Porkchopper from Martin County!"

A: "Yes ma'am. My people, except for the Jupiter Island area, were farming folks, really."

Four teachers pose outside the original Gifford school in about 1950. The school was at U.S. 1 and 39th Street. (Provided by Eddie Hudson from collection of Queenie Phillips)

Students Shared Textbooks in Old Gifford School

*D*ecades before integration, black children in Indian River County traveled to Fort Pierce to go to school. Then, in the 1920s, someone donated land along U.S. 1 for a school in the predominantly black community of Gifford, just north of Vero Beach. Eddie Hudson went to school there in the 1940s.

"It no longer exists there, but it was a frame building that had a big hall down the middle. The classrooms were on either side. The drinking fountain was like a cows' trough."

Q: "And it was sulphur water. Right?"

A: "Yeah. We didn't have running water in Gifford. Either you drilled your well yourself and put your pitcher pump on it or some people in Gifford were able to have an artesian well drilled and they would charge families a small fee to tap into it."

Q: "What did you have?"

A: "Originally, we had our own well. Then when our neighbor had a company drill an artesian well, our father was able to come up with the $50 to tap in."

Q: "But you didn't have running water…"

A: "We did not have inside plumbing at all."

Q: "What was school like?"

A: "We had excellent teachers! The only problem, and I didn't learn that until after the fact, was that the books that we got were always used. The kids in town used the books when they were new."

Q: "You mean the Vero kids?"

A: "The Vero kids, yes. There were never enough books. God rest her soul, Mrs. Bernice Johnson had about 35 kids in her class. She may have had 10 spellers and 15 math books. It hurt her so much that some of us didn't get books to take home. She found out where each one of us lived. Back then, we didn't have street names so we had to describe to her where we lived."

Q: "The streets weren't named?"

A: "No. There were no signs on the streets. Mrs. Johnson was one of the teachers who would find out where you lived. If I lived near you, she would give me a math book to take home and maybe give you a speller. If I had

45

math homework, I'd get it done and then I'd bring that book to you. By that time, you should have your spelling words done and you'd give me the speller."

Q: "What about lunch at school?"

A: "You had to pay for your lunch."

Q: "How much?"

A: "I think it was ten cents a day."

With nine children in the Hudson family, paying for school lunches was out of the question. Their mother would make extra pancakes in the morning and send them to school in a sack.

"When lunch time came we would all gather around!"

A more modern Gifford High School came along in the early 1950s, but unlike Vero Beach High School it didn't have a laboratory or gym at first. But Hudson has happy memories of growing up in Gifford. Kids played marbles and made their own toys, he says.

"We'd make bird traps. We'd take those birds home and clean them. My mother would take the birds and cook a pot of rice, put the birds in it and it would make a meal."

Q: "What kind of birds?"

A: "Any kind we could get! Blue birds, red birds, cardinals, quail."

Q: "Was this in your yard?"

A: "Oh no. We'd go out in the woods. I'm surprised that none of us really got bitten by snakes."

Q: "Were you barefoot?"

A: "Yeah. I went to school barefoot sometimes! But we had fun. I mean, there was no life like it growing up."

Eddie Hudson and one of his brothers used to hunt rabbits, which often congregated in culverts in citrus groves.

"Some guy told us that what we could do was get a big sack, put it on one end of the culvert, and get something like a fishing pole and run it down the other end, and the rabbits would run out and get into the sack. The rabbits, of course, provided meals for us as well. My mother used to put batter on them and fry them like chicken. A couple of years ago, I went out to one of the supermarkets and bought some rabbit and made a rabbit meal out of it. Very delicious!"

Q: "Did it bring back memories?"

A: "Oh yes."

Eddie Hudson, who earned a doctorate in education, retired in 1995 after 34 years as a teacher and administrator in Indian River County.

George Smathers smiles about his lead over incumbent Claude Pepper in 1950 Senate race. (Associated Press)

Did Politician Fool Rural Floridians With Big Words?

*A*n enduring political legend in Florida has it that U.S. Sen. Claude Pepper was defeated, in 1950, because of some big words his challenger, George Smathers, used to mislead backwoods voters. Example: Smathers supposedly accused Pepper of practicing "celibacy" before his marriage. At the time, Zora Neale Hurston was helping Smathers' father, Judge Frank Smathers, write his autobiography. She supported George Smathers. Author Lynn Moylan writes about this in her new book about Hurston's final decade.

"She had this great slogan that she made up for Smathers: you can't make a meal out of Pepper!"

Q: "And that's interesting because Pepper might have been considered more liberal than Smathers."

A: "Well, when you look at the time period, you find that George Smathers was less racist than Claude Pepper. Pepper made speeches promising that he would do nothing to change the Southern customs."

Q: "Like the poll tax?"

A: "Exactly! Another issue that hurt Claude Pepper and that encouraged Hurston to support Smathers was that Claude Pepper was a supporter of Stalin (Soviet dictator)."

Q: "Did Zora's support for Smathers bring in some black votes?"

A: "I would think that it did. She promoted the fact that Smathers was a supporter of the black population being able to attend games at the Orange Bowl. He did believe that integration was something to be desired, but he, like Hurston, felt that it should be done gradually. George Smathers has been criticized for making a speech that he never made."

Q: "Which one was that?"

A: "It was the infamous 'thespian' speech."

Q: "His sister was a 'thespian' in New York, or something like that, Claude Pepper's sister?"

A: "It was really, really awful. When I talked to Bruce Smathers about this, he said what people don't realize is that even though this infamous speech was supposed to have been delivered to the poor backwoods residents of North Florida, for Smathers to have said things like, 'Are you aware that Claude Pepper is known all over Washington, D.C., as a shameless extrovert,' would have been an insult to the businessmen and attorneys and teachers who were also in North Florida. The Miami Herald and other newspapers had people following him around, writing down every single thing that was said. There was not one person who came forward to claim that he made those statements."

Q: "He didn't call Pepper 'Red Pepper?'"

A: "No. Actually, that came from the *Washington Post*. Pepper was going around the country supporting Stalin. *The Washington Post* was upset by that."

Besides consulting Bruce Smathers, who is George Smathers' son, Moylan said she studied Pepper biographies and researched the historical record.

"Hurston has been soundly criticized for supporting Smathers, but when you look at the record, you can understand why she would support Smathers."

Q: "Did she have an effect on the outcome, in your opinion?"

A: "I don't think so."

Q: "She worked with George Smathers' cantankerous father, a Southern conservative. How did that work out?"

A: "Well, the best way I can describe it is working with Judge Smathers to Hurston was like running against the wind of a Category 5 hurricane!"

Q: "That's not what she said!"

A: "No. That's how I described it. According to his son, he had a beastly disposition and was a bigoted Southern man. It was very difficult for him to accept, at first, that Hurston could finish this intellectual task that he could not. As time went on, he began to see that Zora was brilliant."

With his own family, Frank Smathers used to provoke arguments and then cover his ears to shut out responses, Moylan said. He tried the same tactic with Hurston.

"Whenever he would plug up his ears after an argument, she would actually inform him that he would listen to her. She would simply pull his fingers out and go on talking."

Q: "The book was published privately. Do you think she really got into his psyche?"

A: "No. It was not noteworthy."

Q: "Vanity press?"

A: "Oh yes. She did not put her talent into it. He pretty much dictated it to her."

Q: "She was a stenographer, sort of."

A: "Oh yes."

Q: "But she got the job done …"

A: "When nobody else could deal with him!"

Zora Neale Hurston (Florida Archives)

The Miami Jetport would have been carved out of the Big Cypress Swamp. Journalist and author Peter Gallagher captured this image of an elusive panther in a tree at Big Cypress, now a federally protected preserve. (Florida Archives)

Jetport Issue Sparked Environmental Awareness

A t the dawn of Florida's environmental movement in the late 1960s, a mammoth building project was being carved out of Big Cypress Swamp. It was going to be the Miami Jetport, 40 miles from the city. Dade County was buying land for it and got federal funds to build the first runway. Nathaniel Reed, the environmental advisor to Gov. Claude Kirk, said everything was being done quietly and quickly.

"Kirk went down for its inaugural flight. He came back and said, hey, you ought to see this thing. It's really going to transform aviation in South Florida. Bob Padrick, who was a member of the South Florida Water Management District board, called me and said, Boss -- he had a great Southern accent -- Boss, there's nothing but trouble out there. It's going to disrupt the entire water flow pattern."

So Reed went to see it for himself.

"I couldn't believe my eyes!"

The next day Reed met with the governor and told him, "I have grave doubts about the wisdom of this. I know it sounds to you, to the promoting side of you, like a good idea, but let me point out a couple of things. It's really distant from Miami and to get people from the airport to Miami is going to require a high- speed train crossing the Everglades. I think we should stop and think and really make a judgment about whether we really want the state to be involved."

Q: "Would it have replaced the current airport, Miami International?

A: "Well, it would have been a disaster, financially."

Kirk agreed to set up a committee of experts who would study the jetport and possible consequences. Reed also urged the governor to discuss the matter with the U.S. secretary of the interior, Walter Hickel, who knew the area.

"He and Kirk and I had been in the Everglades together for a wild night: a great deal of booze and a great deal of fun. I went to bed but the two of them stayed up and made great friends."

Q: "Telling stories?"

A: "Telling stories endlessly, going out looking for alligators, having a bonny time."

Another federal official, Russell Train, had a home near Reed's on Jupiter Island in Martin County.

"He called me back and said what the hell is this jetport? Why haven't you stopped it? I said it's a little more complicated than that."

The committee wrote 101 questions about the project, which they planned to pose at a meeting called by jetport boosters, including the mayor of Miami, Chuck Hall, and the airport director, Alan Stewart. The mayor was at the podium.

"He read the question and then the answer was, this question is under study. Question number two: he read the question and said this question is under study."

Q: "Don't tell me he did that for all 101 questions!"

A: "At eight, I'd had it! I stood up and said, Mayor, are the next 93 questions going to be answered, this is under study? He said, you are a white militant! Shut up! This is my meeting. You are a white militant! I said whether I'm a white militant or not, I represent the governor of Florida. Are the next 93 questions going to be answered the same way?"
Finally one of the officials told Reed, "We're going to build you a glass house and fill it with butterflies -- it was well known that I had loved collecting butterflies as a youth -- and we're going to give you your own little butterfly net. I said thank you so much! Just answer this one question. Are you going to effectively answer any one of these questions? He said no, they were all under study. There were TV camera men and all the writing press was there. There must have been 80 members of the federal and state government, county government, upstream government, experts in ecology. The room exploded! The mayor and Stewart had an escape route."

Q: "Literally? Out the back door?

A: "Out the back door, into a limousine and gone, saying we took care of those guys!"

Instead, the jetport made front-page news all over the country the next day. That led to a federal review of the project and in 1970 President Richard Nixon cancelled federal funding for the project. The Big Cypress Swamp became a federally protected preserve.

Development, Business and Making a Living

Section 2

A model city at the 1893 Chicago World's Fair, shown here, inspired some Scandinavian immigrants to start a new community in St. Lucie County.

Chicago World's Fair Inspired White City Settlers

*M*illions of visitors were dazzled at the sight of a model city at the 1893 Chicago World's Fair. The buildings were white, the architecture Greek classical. It was called White City and it became the inspiration for a settlement in Florida. N.C. Jorgensen and some friends read about the Chicago exhibit and decided to create a town of the same name. Jorgensen's granddaughter, Dorothy Russ, lives in White City, south of Fort Pierce. Jorgensen and the other early settlers, most of them Danish immigrants, had heard wonderful things about Florida, Russ said.

"They heard stories about how cheap the land was and how the climate was so mild that you could plant two crops a year, and there was lots of game. They chose six men to do some exploring."

Q: "Did they lay the town out to be like the White City at the World's Fair?"

A: "They certainly did. They even dug a basement space where there was going to be a bank, but they found that Florida wasn't the place to have basements!"

Q: "In other words, they hit water before they finished the job!"

A: "My grandfather built a three-story frame hotel and my grandmother did all the cooking for the guests. What happened to it was my grandfather still owned it, and it was vacant. Three of my uncles tore it down and divided the lumber and built their own houses."

Q: "Those early settlers liked to build two-story houses and a lot of the houses have survived. What was the secret of the construction?"

A: "One of the main things was they used that good lumber, heart of pine. The house that Dad and my grandfather built for us to live in is still standing, and the year that it was built was 1934, which had four hurricanes."

Q: "And a bunch of hurricanes since 1934! The house came through unscathed?"

A: "Came through all of them!"

Q: "White City has never been incorporated and it doesn't have street lights and sidewalks …"

A: "It does not."

Q: "Did your grandfather and the other settlers intend for it to be that way?"

A: "They did not. They intended to build a city."

Q: "Your grandfather was a builder and grower. Your grandmother assisted the physician, Dr. Platt, and delivered babies."

A: "My grandmother was just a natural nurse, I suppose. I don't think she had any formal training, but she knew what to do and how to do it. One time a man had to row across the (St. Lucie) river and walk to get my grandmother, who also had to go across the river."

Q: "Did she get there in time?"

A: "She did, and the man was so grateful for her tending his wife that when he went to North Florida where citrus groves had been planted, he brought back some buds for my grandfather so he could start his own grove."

Q: "If somebody had needed to go to a hospital, where would they have gone?"

A: "I never heard anybody even mention a hospital. Fort Pierce did have sort of a hospital."

Q: "Did you ever hear any stories about getting used to the heat and the rain and the critters of Florida?"

A: "I don't remember hearing anybody complain, but I do remember hearing my grandmother say you must get up early and get your work done while it's cool."

Q: "How do you think your grandparents would feel if they came to White City today?"

A: "They would be so amazed! I don't think they could believe their eyes."

Q: "They'd also see some houses that they would recognize."

A: "There aren't a whole lot of them, but there are some."

Bottling 'The Real Thing' In Fort Pierce

*F*orget two-liter plastic for a moment. There was a time when Coke came in six-ounce glass bottles. You remember those little bottles with the skinny necks. William "Pop" Cross ran a Coca Cola bottling plant in Fort Pierce in the 1930s and 40s. Carrie Sue Ray is his daughter.

"My daddy had one truck. They sold so little Coke they took the truck everywhere! My daddy's district went as far north as Winter Beach and as far south as Stuart and west to Yeehaw Junction, and when they went out there it would be an all-day thing because it was all dirt roads and the truck would get stuck! It would be a real ordeal to deliver maybe 10 cases of Coke."

Q: "Were these in the little bottles?"

A: "These were the six-ounce bottles. In the bottling plant, the syrup and the water were up above the bottling part. The bottles came in on a conveyor. You could see the bottles being filled with an ounce of Coke syrup, and the rest with the water and then the cap would be fastened on. There was a man standing at the end of the conveyor belt and he would pick up four bottles, two in each hand, and lay them over a light to make sure the bottles were clean and there was nothing contaminating in them. Those bottles were washed with really hot, hot water. They went on a conveyor through a regular washing process, with really strong soap and a drying process."

Q: "I wonder how many bottles of Coke were produced in a day."

A: "I don't know, but my daddy could have told you exactly how many ounces of syrup they used because they had to use a very strict inventory. My dad could look at the way they had the Coke cases stacked and count them. All of it was six-ounce bottles and they were a nickel, and a carton of Coke was a quarter. At first you had little wooden cartons where you bought six Cokes."

Q: "Do you have any of those?"

This grocery store promotes Coke floats in photo from the early 1960s (Florida Archives)

An early Coca Cola truck in Tampa, probably in the 1920s.
(Florida Archives)

A: "I did, but over the years my things have disappeared. I wish I had all my Coke stuff! I had little trucks with Coke bottles, and of course they made everything -- pencils, clocks, tablets – every kind of advertising thing."

Q: "You were saying that Cokes that just came off the assembly line tasted better."

A: "They were much better. They were still really cold from the cold water that was used to mix it. When I was growing up, I had all the Coke I wanted, which, of course, was not too wonderful health-wise in your later years! We didn't know that. It was just good and we had whatever we wanted."

Q: "Did you have it with every meal?"

A: "No, but I had it in the refrigerator, or I stopped by the Coke plant and got it as it came off the assembly line."

Q: "Was it hard to sell the public on Coke as opposed to other soft drinks?"

A: "I don't think so. Eventually, people came to realize what a good drink it was. At that time, there were places that would buy one case at a time and my daddy would take them one case if that's what they wanted. But eventually, he had four different trucks going west and south and north to sell Coke, and there was one place on the beach. By the time he left there in 1945, we had the big amphibious base and they were selling thousands of cases of Coke. Before that he had to really work to sell to the grocery stores. My mother was not allowed to buy groceries anywhere that they didn't sell Coca Cola. We didn't dare drink anything that wasn't Coca Cola, because there was a Nehi bottling plant here too."

Q: "Brand X!"

A: "Exactly! And we thought it was so good to sneak a Nehi because they came in great big bottles – if your daddy didn't catch you!

Carrie Sue Ray still lives in Fort Pierce.

Coca Cola is promoted in Apalachicola on this 1915 parade float (Florida Archives)

Fellsmere sugar mill shown in this post card from about 1950
(Fellsmere Photo Collection of Clarence F. Korker)

Sugar Mill Thrived During Great Depression

*T*here are some sweet memories in Fellsmere, a small town east of the St. John's Marsh in Indian River County. During the depths of the Great Depression, a brave soul named Frank Heiser overcame all odds, from drainage problems to freezes and hurricanes, and established the town as a center for commercial sugar cane production. He planted sugar cane, built a refinery and marketed the product as Florida Crystals. Heiser, who died in 1961, is credited with keeping Fellsmere afloat during tough economic times. Joel Tyson, a former mayor of Fellsmere, has ties to the town dating back to the 1940s.

"Heiser thought sugar cane would do well here. I don't know what inspired him, but he talked some people into letting him put in an experimental patch of sugar cane. Eventually they put in 17,000 acres of sugar cane!"

Q: "I thought sugar cane needed to have soil with muck in it, like the soil around Lake Okeechobee.'

A: "Well, we're right on the banks of the St. John's River here, the start of the St. John's River. The muck land here is unbelievable! It's a sod farm now."

"At first, they were not refining the sugar here. They would squeeze the cane and cook the juice. Then they shipped it to Louisiana, I think, where they refined it. Well, they decided they needed to do the whole thing right out here."

Q: "You know what it entails, from growing sugar cane to processing. How does it work?"

A: "First of all, when you get ready to harvest sugar cane, you have to burn the fields, to get rid of the extra foliage and so forth that's out there."

Q: "So that people can come in and cut it?"

A: "Exactly right. They had cane cutters from down in the (Caribbean) islands. They could come in and cut the cane, and load it on wagons. They had a railroad track out there, so they would haul the sugar into the mill. Then the sugar cane was squeezed, to get the juice out. Then they would cook the juice to make it like syrup. They had great big centrifugal vats that they put the juice in to spin off the molasses. First you would have brown sugar. If you kept spinning it long enough, you would have pure crystal sugar. The finished product was called Florida Crystals and was shipped to market by rail."

Q: "I guess that was Fellsmere's largest employer…"

A: "During the Depression it was probably one of the largest employers in the country! People would ride the rails -- hobos and so forth – and .there were all kinds of people coming into Fellsmere looking for jobs. Well, anybody who had a job out there would kill to keep the job. The sugar mill worked all during the Depression, never slowed down. It was phenomenal! There were no jobs to be had anywhere in the United States."

Q: "And they were coming to Fellsmere?"

A: "They were coming to Fellsmere from all over the country, because they heard there was a sugar mill where they might be able to get a job."

Q: "Did you ever taste sugar cane from the field?"

A: "We would chew it as kids. It grows in joints, you know. You take those joints and peel the outer bark off. It's real fibrous. You ever chew on a piece of sugar cane?

"I never have."

"Well, it's real juicy. I mean, you would cut it into little cubes and chew it."

In the 1940s, Heiser and his partners sold the company. Sugar cane production in Fellsmere ceased in the 1960s.

Joel Tyson, who is retired from the military, worked 19 years as an overseas consultant.

Woman who just caught some frogs. (Florida Archives)

Frog Legs Boosted
Okeechobee's Economy

*B*efore marshes were drained, frog legs were a major export from Okeechobee County. The Osceola Fish Co. sold fish, of course, but also soft-shelled turtles, marsh rabbits and frog legs. William Hendry's father owned the business.

"He got into the frog business rather by accident. He had several pairs of bullfrogs that he kept in the back yard. Some journalist wrote an article, sort of a tongue-in-cheek article, about 'Hendry's Frog Farm.' Well, this was picked up, apparently, by some Northern newspapers, because it was no time at all before a frog buyer from Chicago came down and wanted to see Hendry's Frog Farm! Of course, my father explained to him that he only had about two pair of frogs but that he could furnish all that the man would desire. That's how he got into the frog business. This was about 1929, and from that time on he was probably, if not the largest frog dealer in South Florida, at least one of them."

Q: "I wonder if people from the North had ever eaten frogs before..."

A: "Frogs were a delicacy in some restaurants, particularly in New Orleans. They were a very popular item at that time. Even in the Depression years, for people who could afford to go out to a nice restaurant, frog legs were usually one of their items of choice, and were fairly expensive, in comparison to other forms of seafood. Frogs were marketed either by cutting the frog in half and selling only the hind legs, or some markets preferred them cut just behind the front legs, leaving a long back on the frog. Depending on the market, that's how my father prepared the frogs for shipping."

"At first, frog hunters brought the frogs in live and we had them in barrels. Well, you can imagine this was a noisy place, with frogs croaking and occasionally escaping out of a barrel and chasing other frogs! These were large bull frogs and they were very plentiful. At that time, Okeechobee had a lot of pond areas. The pastures hadn't been drained. Fact is, most of the pastures were open so that frog hunters could go anywhere freely and have access to the pond and marsh areas. During the Depression years, frog hunting was probably one of the main industries that sustained the economy. People out of work could go frog hunting at night. There was no particular equipment required, of any expense. They would cut cabbage stalks off the sable palms and whittle out a rather large fly swatter, if you will. They would use those just to stun the frog. Others would use what was called a gig. They would use a fish hook and straighten the fish hook and attach them in a circular manner around a piece of wood and attach a long bamboo pole to it. It was almost like a spear, and it would have maybe four or five barbs on the end. They would gig the frogs in that manner. They would retrieve them and put them in a sack and usually hunt all night long or until they had a sufficient catch."

Q: "Do you remember how much your father paid for a bushel of frog legs or whatever it was; a sack of frogs?"

A: "In my recollection, in the late 1930s my father paid, I think, 15 cents a pound, and at the same time fish only brought about three cents a pound. A lot of children would go frog hunting and get extra spending money, because it was easy to do. Course, there were hazards attached. All those marsh areas also had a lot of snakes."

Q: "Did you ever do that?"

A: "I tried it. I just didn't care for it. I did a little commercial fishing, but I didn't care for the frog hunting."

Q: "During the Depression, I bet a lot of frog hunters put some of the frogs on their own tables ..."

A: "Frogs were a delicacy in households, and commercial fishermen would always reserve a few fish back for their dinner table."

Q: "Did you eat frogs and a lot of fish?

A: "We rarely had frog legs. My mother would prepare them when company was coming but, as a household item in our diets we had mostly fish."

William Hendry is a retired circuit judge in Okeechobee.

Elmer Miller and his son, Donald, pose in a grapefruit grove in northeast Florida in this 1930 postcard. (Florida Archives)

Napoleon Aide Introduced Grapefruit to Florida

C itrus historian Paul Driscoll likes to tell people that if Napoleon hadn't met his Waterloo, the grapefruit might never have come to Florida. It had to do with a character by the name of Count Odet Philippe, who served as a surgeon in Napoleon's navy. When Napoleon was defeated by the British, Philippe wound up in the United States. He eventually settled on the west coast of Florida, near the present-day town of Safety Harbor, and became a tree farmer.

"He started his tree farm and wanted to get other species to grow, so he went down to the island of Barbados. Back then, Barbados was also called Paradise Island. While he was there, he found a fruit and didn't know what it was."

Q: "Did he give it the name grapefruit?"

A: "No. The scientific name for grapefruit was *citrus paradisi,* after the fact that Barbados was called Paradise Island."

Q: "I thought citrus was native to China."

A: "Citrus is native to China, but the grapefruit is not known in China. What is known in China is the large, similar looking fruit called the pummelo. Some pummelos were brought to Barbados about 1649 by an English sea captain named Phillip Shaddock. Sometimes they're called the shaddock rather than the pummelo."

Q: "Do they taste like a modern grapefruit?"

A: "They're a very dry fruit but the Chinese like them. The fruit sacs are very individual. You can scrape them and use them in salads. They're not as juicy as a grapefruit."

Q: "But the Chinese still eat them. Do they still raise them?"

A: "Yep. In fact, there was a Chinese man who was raising some south of Stuart. He had about 20 acres of pummelos down there."

Q: "Have you ever eaten pummelos?"

A: "I've tasted them but never used them in my diet. In 1981 two California researchers while doing DNA work discovered that the grapefruit is an accidental crossing of a pummelo and a sweet orange. That probably occurred in the 1700s."

Q: "Where do they think it happened?"

A: "That was in Barbados. Count Philippe took seeds from the grapefruit. He planted a grove in Safety Harbor, which was later owned by a Mr. Duncan. That's how the variety got its name, the Duncan."

Q: "In other words, the regular garden-variety grapefruit is known as the Duncan."

A: "That's the white seedy grapefruit. Probably the only place you can find it now is in specimen gardens. The Duncan also has a characteristic that gives all grapefruit its name. It grows in clumps, so when people looked at the Duncans, they called them grapefruit."

Q: "Because they looked like a clump of grapes!"

The grapefruit industry has taken a beating in recent years, the result of dismal economic conditions and diseases such as canker and greening. Driscoll, who is retired from citrus management, says total acreage of grapefruit grown in Florida has dropped from 146,000 in 1994 to 53,000 at present. That's a decline of about two-thirds. A while back he went to see one of the groves he used to manage.

A: "It was very sad just riding out to the grove and seeing other groves that I'd known most of my working career, seeing them abandoned, nothing but pushed up, bare land. It was very sad and as a native Fort Pierce person, I know three citrus families that were growers for three generations, at least, that aren't in the business today."

Q: "What's your favorite kind of citrus?"

A: "Well, you know, I really made my living growing grapefruit, and I like a good grapefruit as much as any kind!"

Q: "What's the future of grapefruit?"

A: "I don't know what the future's going to be."

Kennedy Groves catalog cover from the 1960s.

'All You Can Drink' Orange Juice Enticed Tourists

*W*hen U.S. 1 was the only major route from the Northeast to Florida, citrus juice stands advertising all-you-can-drink orange juice beckoned to motorists passing through the Indian River region. Citrus grower Ken Kennedy literally grew up at the stand that his parents operated in south Vero Beach.

"They would carry me down there as a baby, because my mom worked down there when I was little. They would put me in bins of fruit. The help was bagging the fruit out of the bins. It was kind of my crib, my baby pen."

Q: "Your stand advertised all the juice you could drink for 10 cents."

A: "That was it! I don't know who actually came up with that, but most of the fruit stands up and down U.S. 1 did that to draw the people in."

Q: "We're talking about tourists. I guess a lot of them had never tasted fresh orange juice."

A: "They hadn't, and it was almost like candy to them. They would stand there and drink cup after cup after cup. We served it up in paper cone cups, and after three or four cups the paper got just droopy, and they'd want another cup. Well, give me another dime and you'll get another cup!"

Q: "You talked to a lot of customers, I imagine, who had never been to this part of the world before."

A: "A lot of times, when U.S. 1 was the only road, they'd stop in and ask how far is Florida! They actually meant how far is Miami."

Q: "Did you say that's not our idea of Florida?"

A: "Yeah! Something like that."

Q: "Did any of them ask questions about the area?"

A: "Yeah, we had a lot of the same customers year after year and they'd just ask about old times, like, 'You mean you didn't have air-conditioning down here. How did you live?'"

Q: "How was the juice made?"

A: "In the late 1940s, my aunt, Clyde Kennedy, made all the juice. She made it in a hand squeezer that was hand cranked."

Q: "You mean somebody had to crank it the whole time she was squeezing?"

A: "That's correct. It was a crank on a pulley. That was before my time. By the time I was coming up in the business, she did have an electric one. In those days, we didn't have the plastic jugs we had in later years, so we would go to the Coca Cola bottling plant and get the gallon glass jugs that the cooked syrup would come in. We'd clean them with Clorox and water. That's what we would use to store the juice in, in Coca Cola ice boxes."

Q: "Did you sell souvenirs?"

A: "Oh yes. When I was a kid, I can remember they sold alligator shoes and handbags. That didn't last but a few years."

Q: "They're pretty pricey now, I think."

A: "Yeah. What we sold in those days was not quite the quality that they have today, if you will. People would walk out in the shoes and they'd get in the rain or something and the shoes would fall apart and they'd bring them back. So that didn't last too long! We sold all the Orange Blossom perfume and Coconut Patties, Pecan Log Rolls, serrated spoons to eat grapefruit with. And the sippers were a big item, the plastic sippers that you would stick in the fruit to get the juice out."

Q: "Do you remember anybody, any of the tourists who were heading to 'Florida,' who actually decided to spend some time here in Vero Beach?"

A: "Oh yes. A lot of people discovered Vero Beach and stopped going down to 'Florida.'"

But some of the U.S. 1 juice stands, including Kennedy's, have faded from the landscape.

A: "As the older generation died off, a lot of the younger generation didn't want to work like that. It was hard work. The older generation, who grew up in the Depression, they were glad to have the work. In the late '80s, we discovered it was probably costing us more in labor to hand out the all-you-can-drink-for-a-dime juice, so we just put a couple of dispensers out on the floor. The people helped themselves and it was free. When they'd walk out, they'd grab a gallon of juice and bag of grapefruit and oranges. We'd probably give away at least a hundred gallons a day, but the sales of the fresh fruit and the gallons of juice were very good."

Kennedy Groves sold the U.S. 1 store in 1991. The company still grows citrus, and packs and ships the fruit from its headquarters in Wabasso. Most of the crop goes to markets in Europe and Japan.

This conch shell promotes Florida. (Florida Archives)

Couple Used to Dive for Elusive Queen Conch

*T*he horse conch, a mean critter that feeds on the delectable meat of the queen conch, is Florida's state shell, but you're much more likely to recognize the queen conch. Its curved pink shell symbolizes fun in the sun. Phil and Joan DeFranco worked as lobstermen when they moved to the Lower Keys from Long Island in the 1970s, but they kept getting conch shells in their lobster traps.

76

"We wound up with so many shells, we had to buy a shell shop to get rid of them!" Phil says. "And then we went diving to get more and more."

Q: "Now the conch is protected, but in those days could you take as many as you could get?"

A: "Twenty a day."

Q: "Tell me where the conch lives and how you take them."

A: "They're usually in 10 to 20 feet of water, on the bottom. They look very much like the bottom because they have growth on their back, just like the surrounding growth."

Q: "In those words, they can hide…"

A: "They hide by not moving. Most people don't recognize them."

Q: "You were telling me they have a foot that they walk with…"

A: "It propels them along the bottom very slowly. They just bump along and if there are things that can be considered predators, they don't move. When they don't move, you can't see them because they blend in so well with the bottom."

Q: "But you had a way of seeing them."

A: "We got used to it."

Q: "You knew where they were or what they looked like…"

A: "Well, we also knew that they were usually inshore of a pile of rocks."

Q: "When was the season? Was it year round?"

A: "Year round. No off-season."

Q: "They were always there, always available and you could always bring them in?"

A: "Weather permitting!"

Q: "What was the biggest or best conch you ever brought in?"

A: "Probably it was about 14 inches long."

"It was one that we grew in our canal," Joan said.

"If a conch had a chip in it, nobody would buy it, so we put it in our own canal," Phil said. "The canal had a wall of stone so the conch couldn't climb out. In several weeks in the canal, conchs would grow bigger and bigger than they possibly could in the ocean."

"They'd get a beautiful color," Joan said.

"In the canal there were probably more plankton and algae as the food source," Phil said. "In the canals the conchs really thrived. If it had a chip in it, the chip would mend and then we would take it, and in the way of all conchs, it would wind up on the shelf."

Q: "The shelf and the dinner table!"

A: "Selling them to tourists."

Q: "How much would you get for a good queen conch?"

A: "Twelve to 15 dollars."

Q: "Did you remove the meat from it yourself?"

A: "You freeze the shell overnight and then the meat slides right out."

Q: "So people who say you have to drill a hole in the shell are wrong?"

A: "You don't do that. It damages the shell."

"He made the best conch fritters around," Joan said. "Any time we had company he had to make the conch fritters for everybody."

Joan and Phil DeFranco operated this shell shop in the Lower Keys.

Q: "In a three-year period, you brought in probably 1,000 conchs, so it was a good little business ..."

A: "It wasn't much money making, but it was fun."

Q: "I thought when you held a conch up to your ear, you would hear the ocean, but I'm holding this milk conch up to my ear and I don't hear anything."

A: "The large shells with thin construction sound like roaring, because of the vibrations."

Q: "So it's not the ocean."

A: "No, unfortunately."

Q: "I bet every tourist who came into your shop ..."

A: "They all put them up to their ear."

79

Q: "Did you tell them the truth?"

A: "I just let them do it, and took their picture."

Joan had a close call under water one time, but she and Phil remember the incident differently.

"My wife didn't have enough weight on her belt, so I put a couple of pounds of weight on," Phil said. "She went down and picked up a conch and then couldn't come back up. Luckily, I was looking down and saw her struggling. She wouldn't let go of the conch, and she didn't know enough to take off the belt and just drop it. I went down and helped her up."

"That's not the way it went," Joan said. "I had the conch in my hand and was on my way up and he said, here, take this other conch because I see another one down there. When I took his conch that's when I started to go back down and couldn't come up!"

Joan and Phil DeFranco are retired in Vero Beach now. They do some shelling on Melbourne beaches and usually stay out of the ocean.

Ross Allen's reptile show attracts attention at 1964 New York World's Fair.
(Florida Archives)

Selling Snakes: It's How 2 Sisters Made Pocket Money

*B*efore Disney, Florida tourist attractions were heavy on gator wrestling and monkey jungles. One of the best known was the Ross Allen Reptile Institute at Silver Springs in Ocala. Ross Allen opened his snake farm in 1929 and promoted it endlessly. Several Tarzan movies starring Johnny Weissmuller were filmed at Silver Springs and Allen sometimes worked as a stand-in for Weissmuller. He always needed a steady supply of snakes, both for research and for tourists who would buy them as live souvenirs. Two sisters who grew up on their parents' dairy near Moore Haven, west of Lake Okeechobee, used to catch and sell snakes to him. Debbie Click Paschal says that's how they made their spending money.

Becky Click Choate says, "We caught what we called chicken snakes, rat snakes, king snakes, mud snakes, and my brother, he was braver than the rest of us so he would catch moccasins or rattlesnakes. We did catch ground rattlers occasionally."

"Poisonous snakes were really against the rules," her sister said. "Our parents really didn't want us messing with the poisonous ones.'

Q: "You captured them live, of course, and delivered them to Ross Allen live..."

A: "Yes, and we had a horse named Speedy. Debbie and I would use him to reach holes up in big trees. Debbie would stand up on back of the horse and brace herself against me while she reached up into a hole where there might be a chicken snake."

Q: "And just stick her bare hand in there?"

A: "No. There were certain trees that maybe a limb had died and it left a cavity in the tree, and then when it would rain it would fill with water. We would take a stick and poke down into the hole and you could tell by the feel whether there was a snake in there or not. But there was one particular tree that we called the grape tree or the snake tree and it wasn't either one. It was a cypress tree that had a huge grape vine. We could climb up the vine and get onto the limb which was at least 12 feet above the ground. We would sit on the limb and poke into the hole. If it felt like a snake was in it, we just kept poking until the snake got irritated with us and then it would come out... Here you are, at least 12 feet above the ground and the snake comes out and stares you in the face, and you just have to freeze! Once he came out, he would generally start climbing up the tree. You would wait until his head was far enough up and then grab it and throw it to the person below."

Q: "Debbie, how much did Ross Allen pay for, let's say, a good-size king snake?"

A: "Well, they generally charged by the foot, maybe ten cents a foot."

"I know for a nice chicken snake we'd get a dollar or a dollar and a half."

"Sometimes as high as two dollars."

"Yes, we hit it big time!"

Man Sold Baby Gators to Tourists for $5 Each

*T*hink of old-time Florida souvenirs and maybe you'll remember a painted coconut or a ceramic ashtray shaped like the Sunshine State. Then there were the living keepsakes. Paul Hunter of Jensen Beach grew up on his grandparents' farm in Lake Worth. He milked cows, hunted rabbits and went to school barefoot until he was 12. His grandfather was known as Palm Beach County's strawberry king. The fruit was prized by tourists and locals alike. Paul had something to offer winter visitors too: recently hatched alligators from a nearby drainage canal.

"I would go out at night with a flashlight and when I'd find a little baby alligator I'd catch him and bring him home. If it was the right time, during the late tourist season, there would be tourists interested in buying them."

Q: "When were alligators hatching?"

A: "I think they started hatching in about February or March, April. They would make their nests during the late winter and they would hatch in about two or three weeks. Then there'd be little alligators around."

Q: "How big were they when they came out of the shells?"

A: "Oh, nine or ten inches, I guess."

Q: "Did you know where the nests were?"

A: "No, I never saw a nest. I didn't know they were there until I saw little alligators swimming in shallow water where I could go in and get them."

Q: "Did the mother alligator ever try to intervene?"

A: "I don't know. What I understand now is they're very protective. Why I didn't get caught I'll never know! I never was charged by one that I know of!"

Q: "You would have known!"

A: "I think so!"

Q: "How did you catch the baby alligators without getting scratched?"

A: "You sneak up on 'em with a flashlight and blind them and grab them by the neck and lift them out of the water. If you hold onto them by the neck, they can't scratch you or bite you."

Q: "What did you do with them before you sold them?"

A: "I just kept them in a tub at home and maybe fed them some scrap or something now and then, and some tourists would come out to the farm. They heard I had baby alligators, and they would give me five bucks for one. That was a lot of money! A lot of money!

Q: "Did any of the tourists ever tell you what they did with the alligators?"

A: "No, but I heard about alligators in the sewers in New York City!"

Q: "So you made five dollars per alligator."

A: "That was more money than I could make for anything else in two or three months, and I usually would give part of it to my mother. That was part of our income. That was a good living! When I was 12 or 14, I would take my shotgun, my fishing pole, get in my boat and paddle down the canal and be gone for a couple of days. That's the way we lived."

Q: "Would you come back with rabbits, maybe?"

A: "Maybe I'd not bring anything back! We shot some big rattlesnakes on the farm.'

Q: "Did you eat the meat?"

A: "Yes. It was good. My mother was one of those kinds of people, anything I would bring home and clean, she would cook. Well, I thought I had her stumped one time. I brought back home a great big old water moccasin that I actually caught while I was fishing. I thought, well, I've got her stumped now. When she sees that I'm cleaning it, she'll tell me to throw it away. Nope, she cooked it, and I had to take the first bite and I couldn't do it, so we threw it away. It smelled bad. Rattlesnake smells good.

Q: "What does it taste like?"

A: "It's white meat, very soft and a little bit sweet."

Q: "Do you remember a really big one?"

A: "Yes. We had a path through the palmettos and one day my mother hollered at me to bring the gun. There was a rattlesnake all the way across the path – it measured just over six feet long – and it had just swallowed a whole rabbit."

Q; "So did you have rattlesnake meat that night?"

A: "We did! But we didn't eat the rabbit.'

Paul Hunter joined the Marines during World War II and became a pilot. He also served in Korea and Vietnam, and retired as a major in 1969.

Waldo Sexton, left, and his son-in-law John Tripson at the entrance to Tripson's Dairy
(Sexton Family Collection, Archive Center, Indian River County Library)

'Mom and Pop' Dairies a Vanishing Breed

*T*here used to be numerous locally owned dairies on the Treasure Coast, but they started fading away when convenience stores sprouted on every corner in the 1970s. One of the best-known "mom and pop" dairies was Tripson's Dairy. The legendary developer Waldo Sexton started it in 1922 in Vero Beach. One of Sexton's grandsons, Mark Tripson, started working in the dairy when he was in high school in the 1960s. He was happy when glass bottling gave way to plastic.

"We were proud when we started using plastic. It made it a lot easier, and it's easier on housewives. They didn't have to bring the bottle back. They always had a deposit on the bottle. People complained about the glass gallon bottles being so heavy."

Q: "How many bottles of milk would Tripson's Dairy bottle in an average day?"

A: "Oh, we probably put up, say, 200 cases of gallons (bottles) and two hundred cases of half gallons. That would be 1,500 or 1,800."

Q: "Virtually all of them were delivered in those Tripson's Dairy trucks ..."

A: "Little trucks. They were funky looking little milk trucks. At one point we had 35 of them on the road. We had a little substation in Fort Pierce. We'd take a semi load of milk there and they'd distribute it from down there."

Q: "What jobs did you do in the dairy, Mark?"

A: "Oh, I started out as bottle washer. We had a bottle washing machine. You had to load it and unload it. It was about 150 degrees, so it was always hard to get people to stand there, but me being young and dumb ..."

Q: "Was this when you were in high school, maybe?"

A: "Yeah. I didn't have much of a choice!"

Q: "Did you wear gloves?"

A: "No. You never hire a man who wears gloves. He'd always be taking them off to smoke cigarettes."

Q: "So you were the chief bottle washer ..."

A: "A long time! Finally we got somebody else to do that. It seems like I always filled in when somebody got sick or was on vacation, so I ended up knowing everybody's jobs."

Q: "Did you milk the cows?"

A: "Oh yes. You had to do that twice a day every day, just two 12-hour shifts when you're milking!"

Q: "Because you start at what time, 3 o'clock or so?"

A: "Everybody thinks you do, but we had to adjust our milking to when the semis would pick the milk up. A lot of times we'd milk at 9 and 9. We'd get through about 1 in the morning or 1 in the afternoon."

Q: "And there were no days off; there were no vacations, there were no holidays from milking!"

A: "Cows don't know about holidays! They don't even know about Daylight Savings! I still don't like Daylight Savings, because you have to adjust your clock. Well, cows don't care. They go by the sun anyway."

Q: "Is there any trick to milking a cow?"

A: "Not that I can think of. It's not hard. It's automated. It's an art knowing when they're through milking!"

Q: "What was the most popular product?"

A: "I think the chocolate milk."

Q: "It came from brown cows. Right?"

A: "That's how you could tell! The last couple years we had the school milk (contract), the kids at school could choose either whole milk, low-fat milk or chocolate milk. I think they then had 10,000 kids in the (county) schools. We produced about 9,000 chocolate milks for them by the second week of school. It was low-fat. Somebody said it was dietetic. Well, I said, yeah, but we put a half pound of sugar per gallon to make it sweet enough to drink!"

Q: "It was a tough business, wasn't it? Physically tough."

A: "Yeah, it was a young man's sport, because it was demanding. The bottling part we did six days (a week) for a long time, then five days. When they got refrigeration, they quit delivering on Sunday."

Q: "Of course, that was before your time…"

A: "Pretty much. When I was really young, they had refrigeration to chill the milk down until they bottled it, but the trucks weren't refrigerated. We had a 10-foot by 12-foot ice maker. You'd take a snow shovel with snow ice and shovel it on the milk so they could deliver it. On a hot summer day we'd go get in the ice makers!"

Q: "What's your most treasured memory of the dairy business?"

A: "Treasured memory?"

Q: "If you have one."

A: "I miss making eggnog. We made eggnog from Thanksgiving to Christmas. For some reason it always grabbed me to make the eggnog. We bought pails of mix that had the nutmeg and the flavoring. You just added milk and a lot of sugar and a lot of cream. I always felt the more cream you added, the better it tasted."

Tripson's Dairy closed about 30 years ago. Mark Tripson and his family still live in the original Sexton homestead on the dairy property in Vero Beach.

Entrance to the turnpike, originally known as the Sunshine State Parkway, at Fort Pierce in 1959 (Florida Archives)

Turnpike a 'Godsend' When it Opened in '57

*U*ntil the turnpike and interstate highways were built, road trips up and down Florida's peninsula could be painfully long. In 1947, Victor Gacy, now of Vero Beach, was a University of Florida freshman from Miami.

"I could have gone to the University of Miami, which was only five minutes away, but I decided on Gainesville. I had a beat-up old car. The first trip I made, it took us a day and half to get there. U.S. 1 was two lanes. We had to go through every little town on the east coast: Fort Lauderdale, West Palm,

Stuart. I can remember going along the Indian River in the fall. The sulphur smell was predominant."

Q: "You said you were in a beat-up car. What kind of car?"

A: "It was a Hudson Terraplane, 1937 vintage. In Gainesville, I sold that car for $50. I got $10 down and never saw the fellow that bought it again."

Q: "He and the car were both long gone?"

A: "Thank goodness! The car was about to fall apart."

Q: "What kind of speed were you able to go?"

A: "Probably about 35 to 40 mph."

Q: "So Miami to Gainesville was about a 300-mile trip?"

A: "365 miles! In probably October we had a hurricane which closed down (Highways) 441 and 27 around the lake. Then we could only use U.S. 1."

Q: "Did you ever have car trouble with that old car?"

A: "Well, I didn't use that car much. After that first Christmas, there were other people in my group who had cars. On occasion we'd hitchhike, which was safe in those days. One trip stands out in my mind. We got a ride in a laundry truck in West Palm, around 30 miles, so that was pretty comfortable."

Q: "You got to lie down among the sheets and towels?"

A: "Dirty laundry!"

Q: "At least it was wheels."

A: "It helped to get us home …. I remember there was a fence law to keep the cattle off the road."

Q: "You never hit a cow on the road, but you had a fraternity brother who did something like that."

A: "He was a fellow from Orlando coming back Sunday night to Gainesville. He hit a cow or a deer. It peeled the hood of the car right back like a sardine can and peeled off the roof. The car was full of blood. The bystanders thought the person was injured badly, but it turned out he walked away from the car. It was blood from the animal!"

Q: "What highway was that on?"

A: "That would have been 441."

Q: "Back before the fence law was in full effect, I guess."

A: "Well, there was probably a lot of territory that wasn't fenced in that should have been."

Q: "The law took hold gradually, I guess. Cattlemen really opposed it."

A: "Definitely! They liked to roam their herds. When they were limited to their own property, the cows would eat the grass, especially the good grass, and wouldn't have much else. In the old days they would roam the prairie and be well fed, and also you could walk them to market, so to speak."

Q: "Those days came to an end, and the cows had to stay home on their own pastures!"

A: "That's correct. It was a lot safer because I'm sure many other accidents happened prior to the fence law. I don't have any idea how expensive fencing was in those days. It was probably a good bit."

Gacy was out of college when the turnpike opened in 1957. His work in citrus required him to drive all over the state.

"The turnpike was really a godsend, because you could then go 50 miles an hour or so. It made life a lot easier."

Q: "It made getting there a lot quicker too!"

A: "Yes, and more time to go to the beach."

Space shuttle Columbia rising from the launch pad at Cape Canaveral (Florida Archives)

Florida's Role in Space Flight Predicted a Century Ago

C ape Canaveral has been at the epicenter of America's space program for more than half a century. Even in 19th century fiction, Florida was seen as the place from which space flights would be launched. Historian and author Robert Taylor teaches courses about the history of the space age.

"When Jules Verne wrote his novel, 'From the Earth to the Moon,' he put his first space launch platform near Tampa."

Q: "Just the wrong coast!"

A: "Beginning around 1950 Central Florida would be the center for American space efforts."

Q: "Why was Cape Canaveral selected?"

94

A: "Initially, America's rocket work was done in New Mexico, but there were problems with security. If you launched a missile out over the ocean, if something goes wrong it falls in the ocean. There were surveys of sites, some in Georgia. Eventually the Canaveral area proved to be perfect: fairly isolated, good transportation, and pre-existing military installations. The first actual launch was in 1950."

Q: "1950? I was thinking more like the end of the '50s."

A: "No. It was unmanned, but it was 1950."

Q: "Was it successful?"

A: "Yes."

Q: "But then, there wasn't anything significant done until after Sputnik ..."

A: "Well, Sputnik of course was the catalyst. The Russians, our arch-enemies in the Cold War, orbited a satellite that sped across the United States every 90 minutes. It was a direct challenge to the American idea of its own technological superiority."

Q: "What did the space race do to Brevard County?"

A: "Oh, it was just an explosion! People came from all over the country. The population doubled, it doubled again, doubled again. There were stories of rocket engineers living in tool sheds, sleeping in drainage pipes because there was no housing. Little towns like Cocoa Beach became internationally famous. It was an economic engine that seemingly would have no end."

Q: "But then, when Apollo ended, things changed."

A: "Well, there were already budget cuts coming in for manned space even before Neil Armstrong and Buzz Aldrin landed on the moon. The last several Apollo missions to the moon were actually cancelled, for budget reasons. The hardware was later used in the Skylab program. They were supposed to go, I believe, as high as Apollo 20. Congress approved the shuttle program when one of the Apollo lunar missions was ongoing. The astronauts walking on the moon were told that Congress approved the

95

shuttle. However, it took quite a bit of time to develop the shuttle. The first one didn't fly until 1981."

Q: "And then it had some setbacks after that, of course."

A: "The shuttle proved to be one of the most complicated, if not the most complicated, machine humans have ever built, which meant there was more that could go wrong. Quite possibly, more was expected of it than it could deliver. Of course, we had the setback of the Challenger accident."

Q: "On balance, would you say that the shuttle program was a success?"

A: "Yes, I would. It did what it was designed to do: gave us access to low earth orbit and made possible the construction of the International Space Station."

Q: "What do you think is going to be next for space?"

A: "This is a huge question. We are, in the U.S, I think, at one of those watershed moments when we have to decide what our role in space will be. Our goals, which we set out even before Sputnik, were to build a space shuttle, have a space station and go to the moon. Well, we've done those things. What now? I think that we have to maintain our manned space efforts. I think that a country is judged by its willingness to take risks. Even if we decide to scale back, other countries are going ahead.

Robert Taylor is a department chair at Florida Institute of Technology in Brevard County.

Alma Lee Loy worked with the late banker Robert Spillman on
a plan to bring a university to Indian River County. A portion
of Highway A1A is dedicated in Spillman's memory.
(Photo by Janie Gould)

John's Island Once Eyed
as University Site

I n the early 1960s developer Fred Tuerk had several thousand acres
of jungle on his hands on the barrier island in Indian River County.
Tuerk offered to give the land to the state, which was planning a new
university. Community leader Alma Lee Loy helped prepare the local
proposal. A young banker named Bob Spillman had a key role, but it ended
in tragedy. Loy said the state's deadline was approaching quickly.

"There was a real short deadline and the idea, just the idea, of bringing a college to this community was very intriguing. We also had the beginning of what we all know as the state college in Fort Pierce, but it was just beginning. Everybody's looking out for themselves, and Fred Tuerk, particularly, he was a developer. He envisioned a university here. We submitted the proposal and the Board of Regents liked it, so we invited them here."

Q: "To look at the land?"

A: "To look at the land. Of course we could hardly find the land, because it was complete jungle, and I do mean jungle, so the day before they arrived, Mr. Tuerk and some of the gentlemen who worked for him went through and took these little sand roads and made them just a little bit bigger so we could get a vehicle through there."

Q: "There were no utilities, there was no nothing!"

A: "This was raw land, and raw jungle, like we used to have up and down the beach. Anyway, we showed them all the wonderful things and told them how wonderful Vero Beach and Indian River County were."

Q: "How did they seem to react?"

A: "I think it was mixed. Number one, they loved the idea that somebody was going to give them the land! Number two, it was quite remote, and of course Indian River Shores was just barely budding as a new community. But they were nice to us, they really were. They took all of the sites and ranked them and they let us know that we were in the top ranking, and please submit a final proposal."

Q: "This was for the University of Central Florida?"

A: "It didn't even have a name but it turns out the University of Central Florida was the university they were talking about. We had such a short period of time between the time they said you're on the list, please complete the final questions. We did and made all those copies you have to make. We had no way to get it to them in Tallahassee. We didn't have fax machines back then. It had to be hand carried, so Bob Spillman, anxious as he was and smart as he was, was also a pilot. He said, 'I will fly this proposal up there and make sure it's there on time,' which he did."

On his return flight, Bob Spillman's small plane crashed in North Florida and Spillman was killed.

A: " Naturally, we didn't believe it. We held out hope until we found out by the end of that day that he was killed. It was such a tremendous shock to this whole community, and you know, I've been thinking whatever happened with our proposal? I don't have any idea what happened after that day, because I don't think any of us really cared. We had lost a wonderful friend. We had lost a community leader. We had lost a young man. Bob Spillman was 35 years old! Fred Tuerk suffered like the rest of us because he had learned to admire this young man who was coming up."

Q: "A few years later Tuerk sold his land to the developers of John's Island."

A: "Things work for the best. If you're just patient, the right things will come at the right time, and I think that's what happened in this situation. John's Island and all the people who have come to live there have been marvelous, marvelous to this county."

Q: "And we have a state college after all!"

A: "Oh yes we do and we're proud of that too. Indian River State College has come a long way."

A monument near the Bethel Creek House notes that Spillman died in service to his community. A portion of Highway A-1-A is named the Robert C. Spillman Memorial Highway."

"Every time I go by, I think about Bob."

The University of Central Florida opened in Orlando in 1968. It was originally called Florida Technological University. Now, with more than 56,000 students, it ranks among the nation's largest universities.

Wildlife

Section 3

Alligator eggs hatching (Harry Hill Collection, Florida Archives)

Husband-Wife Team Trapped 'Nuisance Gators'

hen swamps became subdivisions on the Treasure Coast, the state's licensed alligator trapper had plenty to do. For 20 years, Tommy Gore Jr. and his wife, Sue, captured wandering gators, sometimes as many as 40 in one week.

"It was always an alligator in someone's yard or in their swimming pool or in their lake, eating their dog. During those days you were not allowed to kill the alligator. Eventually, the state would require us to kill the gator to process the meat and hides, but we could not do that until we brought the gator home."

Q: "I'm going to ask how you catch an alligator and I'm sure the answer could be, 'very carefully.'"

A: "Very carefully, yes. My wife probably caught the largest alligator that any woman ever caught in South Florida. I got a call from a lady in hysterics: 'Mr. Gore, Mr. Gore, come quick. Your wife needs you!' So I get to the lady's house in Port St. Lucie and I see a five-foot alligator tied across the tailgate of my pickup truck. I looked over and I said now what in the world does my wife need with me with a five-foot alligator! She handles that every day by herself. She says, 'No, Mr. Gore. The one down there tied to the tree.' I looked and there's a 12-foot, 9-inch alligator that my wife got out of the water by herself. She had him wrapped up and tied his mouth taped shut and couldn't do anything with him at that point. The alligator weighed 800 or 900 pounds! She says, 'I threw the bait to him. He swallowed the bait down. I pulled him up, and then I made my helper hold the line and I lassoed him around the neck. I tied the other end of the rope to the truck. I backed the truck down, pulled him up on the bank and then made my helper hold the line tight.' She says she threw her helper's shirt over the gator's eyes so he wouldn't see her when she jumped, and then she jumped on top of the alligator!

Q: "Oh my gosh!"

A: "Just like it was normal routine!"

Q: "There was a time not that long ago when alligators were almost extinct in Florida."

A: "Well, when we were growing up, running the marshes in western St. Lucie County, we didn't see very many alligators. Like you say, they were on the extinct list. Then they were on the endangered list, and then they rebounded to overpopulation, which probably wasn't overpopulation on the alligator's side. It was overpopulation by people, draining the wetlands and the alligators having no place to go."

Q: "How many gators do you suppose you've trapped, you and your wife?"

A: "In the thousands! We've caught as many as 40 in one week."

Q: "Probably in the month of May, when they are moving?"

A: "May, June and July, and then again in August when they begin to hatch out. There's always a problem with children thinking the exposed eggs would be neat to approach, not realizing what the mama alligator is going to do. That's the only time I've ever considered an alligator really dangerous."

Q: "Like a mama bear?"

A: "She's going to protect those eggs. I've had to climb many a six-foot tall chain-link fence because I didn't realize that mama was guarding that nest. She approaches you very rapidly."

Q: "She's not happy!"

A: "Not happy at all."

Q: "Have you ever been bitten, scratched, whipped by a gator tail?"

A: "I've been bitten once by a little baby alligator. Even that size is extremely painful. When he bites you he won't release his grip."

Q: "So what did you do?"

A: "Just kept tapping him on the head. After a while he's going to try to bite you again, so get your hand out while you can. But on the larger alligator, forget it. An alligator goes into a violent spin when he bites something. He rolls. If he gets you by the hand, you better hope the hand goes. Just the hand."

Tommy Gore, now retired, also worked as a state agent for treasure salvage operations.

Hunters carry alligator captured from Lake Kissimmee in this 1870 image. (Florida Archives)

The Jones family homestead, settled in the 19th century along the Indian River, is now owned by Indian River County. (Photo by Janie Gould)

Pioneer Fisherman Recalls 'Gator Trout' and Salt-Water Termites

A fellow named Seaborn Jones settled along the river in Indian River County well before the turn of the 20th century. His grandson, lifelong waterman Richard Milton Jones, was 91 in 2010 and still living on the family homestead along Jungle Trail. Jones said his father sold fish to feed workers who were building Henry Flagler's Florida East Coast Railway.

"He got two cents a pound for 'em."

Q: "Was it mostly mullet?"

A: "Yeah, it was all mullet – cheap fish – millions of them were in there. There ain't hardly any there any more. The river is polluted so bad that the fish have left it, those that haven't been caught."

Q: "So is that how your father really started in the fishing business, by feeding Flagler's crews?"

A: "That was one of the main reasons for being here. He fished a lot, cast nets and gill nets."

Q: "Was there a trick to being a successful fisherman? What was your secret?"

A: "The weather, the duration of the winds. Our speckled trout, they really knew a lot about being caught. You had to be kind of a specialist to catch them in here."

Q: "How come?"

A: "They fed at certain times of the day. They fed at the tides, the winds, the temperatures. The big trouts, the ones we called the ol' gator trouts, any that were 10 or 12 pounds were pretty sharp. I'd put gill nets around them. A lot of times they learned to lay down on the nets."

Q: "So they wouldn't get tangled up in them?"

A: "That's right. I caught a 14 pounder out of this river. I think the record's 18 pounds, out of the Fort Pierce Inlet."

Q: "Were you a shrimper too?"

A: "Well, I caught shrimp off my dock, under a light. We used to get these northwest winds, and it'd turn cool. These 'ol red shrimp used to come through the Ponce de Leon Inlet around New Smyrna. They'd come down the waterway. We used a light out at night and here they'd come with their eyes shining. We caught a lot of 'em with dip nets. I sold those mostly for people to fish with. The bigger ones we'd pull the heads off. We sold them to restaurants. Two dozen for a quarter!"

Jones Pier is a landmark on Jungle Trail on the barrier island north of Vero Beach.

Q: "Tell me about the original pier. Did your grandfather build it?"

A: "I don't know who built the first one. We had a contractor here two or three times. I done a lot of the work on it myself. Them PVC posts you see out there are filled with cement, two bars of steel. And they don't come out in a hurricane!"

Q: "But the original dock, can you tell me about it?"

A: "Cabbage palms! It was built on the trunks of cabbage palms. At that time we didn't have those teredos in the river like there are now. They call 'em salt water termites. That's a bug that eats the wood. When they opened up the (Sebastian) Inlet, they let 'em in, and boy, they've been here ever since. They're very destructive to any wooden boat if you don't take care of it. We didn't have any Fiberglas boats then. They were all wooden boats, mostly cypress, some pine. They'd always start to eat in the keel, and boy, they'd eat that keel up in you'd didn't pull the boat out."

Q: "Did the salt water termites damage your dock?"

A: "Yeah, they ate them old pilings. They ate everything I put in except PVC!"

Q: "Are they still out there in the river?"

A: "Yeah, they're still out there."

Q: "But most boats aren't wooden anymore."

A: "No, you can't hardly sell a wooden boat."

Q: "And the bugs haven't found a way to bite into Fiberglas, right?"

A: "They can't handle that! They're no good on PVC either!"

Jones was chatting on the front porch of his house facing Jungle Trail and the river.

Q: "Were you born here, in this house?"

A: "I was born in Winter Beach."

Q: "Across the river."

A: "My mother went on over when she was pregnant, to have me. I went over inside and came back outside!"

Richard Milton Jones died March 26, 2011 at the age of 92. He sold his property to Indian River County for preservation as a historic site and park.

Historic image shows people surrounding slaughtered manatee (Florida Archives)

Author Traces Changing Views
about Manatees

L ong before manatees became an endangered species, they were known as sea cows because of their meat. Craig Pittman, author of the book "Manatee Insanity," says one veteran of the Seminole Wars described it as "better than the best Tennessee beef."

"Settlers in the Miami area, Coconut Grove, liked to make a dish called gypsy stew. Manatee was one of their favorite ingredients."

Q: "They were easy to catch. Is that right?"

A: "They could be. They'd string a net across an area where manatees were known to frequent and trap them in there. They had this thing known as a bang stick that they could kill them with."

Q: "When did perceptions in Florida about manatees start to change?"

A: "The first law that was passed to protect them was passed in 1893 by a fellow named Frederick Morse, who was a state representative from what became Miami. He passed this law through the Legislature that said you could only kill manatees for scientific purposes and even then you had to get a permit from your county commission, and if you didn't you faced a fine of $500 and six months in jail. The law was loosely enforced and the killings continued but that was the first sign that people were concerned that manatees might be disappearing. The real revolution in attitudes, though, came in the late '60s and early '70s when a researcher named Woody Hartman came down from Cornell to complete his doctorate by doing an in-depth study of manatees, literally, in that he was the first scientist to actually don a mask and flippers and go swimming with them. Woody's research was partly financed by "National Geographic" magazine. He then wrote a story about what he found. That led to Jacques Cousteau coming to Crystal River to do a special called "Forgotten Mermaids." That was the first time people really took a good long look at manatees and understood what they were and were intrigued by them. As a result, tourists began showing up at Crystal River and saying they wanted to see the manatees.

Q: "Are you talking about the West Indies manatee and is it native to Florida? I didn't think it was."

A: "The West Indies manatee is native to Florida. Fossils have been found around Blue Springs that date back millions of years. William Bartram, in his travels through Florida in the 1700s, documented seeing manatees around Blue Springs."

Q: "I wonder why it's known as the West Indies manatee.

111

A: "I think that's the first place that scientists encountered it. Columbus saw manatee and described in his logbook that "mermaids were not nearly as attractive as they were supposed to be!"

Q: "Have you found any estimates or illustrations to show how plentiful manatees were at one time?

A: "Nobody knows. In fact, one of the reasons manatees were put on the endangered species list was that nobody knew how many there were. The estimate now is that there are about 5,000 swimming around Florida."

Q: "That's all?"

A: "Yes. That's actually more than they found in the early 2000s, when there about 3,000."

Q: "How are manatees tracked?"

A: "By radio transmitter attached to their tails. The thing that makes manatees so appealing is that they are an endangered species that you can see. They show up at people's backyard docks. They show up at state parks."

Q: "They almost look like they're smiling!"

A: "In the book, I describe them as being sort of like hippies. They have a strong sex drive. They're non-violent. They actually greet each other with something that looks like a kiss. They're staunch vegetarians. Their only known predator is man."

Q: "Manatees went from being sea cows, a food source, to what some might say, a sacred cow."

A: "That's a good comparison. They have this peculiar look about them. There are at least two documented instances at Homasassa Springs State Park when elderly visitors were so entranced by the manatees they saw swimming below them that they leaned over and their dentures fell out."

In recent years, the manatee and its protected status have been the focus of legal and political battles between environmentalists and boaters as well as builders of docks and waterfront homes.

"Things have somewhat settled down. Waterfront development hasn't been stopped by the regulations. It's been stopped by the economy. I think that may be the real reason for the lull."

Craig Pittman covers environmental issues as a reporter for the St. Petersburg Times.

This statue of a manatee is prepared for permanent display in Key West. (Florida Archives)

Man "tonguing" for oysters from barge (Florida Archives)

Pioneer Descendant Remembers Cold-Weather Oysters

O ysters from the Indian River used to be the mainstay of local diets. When Edward Summerlin settled in St. Lucie (now St. Lucie Village, north of Fort Pierce) in 1887, he grew pineapples and looked to the river for green turtles, fish and oysters. Polly Summerlin Moore is his granddaughter.

"Through the years our family has always gotten oysters. Usually it's a little after Christmas when the oysters really get good, what they call fat. In the summer they say they're poor. A lot of them get a little milky liquid in them instead of the nice clear liquid that the good oysters have. So they have a

114

season when they go for oysters. They always look forward to it and I do too!

When Polly was growing up, her father, Ben Summerlin, often took her brother and her out on the river to get oysters.

"Sometimes it was cold weather, and of course he put us in the water and he stayed in the boat to do what they call "cull" the oysters. We would put the oysters up there and then he would knock off all the extra shell and just keep the better oysters. When you knock the shells into the river, that leaves it for creating more oysters."

Q: "Is there a particular place where you went?"

A: "At that time you could go anywhere away from civilization, which was right along the shore here (St. Lucie Village). Where I remember them going most was along the northwest coast of the river, and there were oyster bars over in the cut too. It was very easy to get them except in cold weather. My father liked big oysters and it seemed there were more big oysters in deep water, so my brother and I would be ducking down to pick up oysters we'd find with our feet. We'd get completely wet with our heads under the water."

Q: "In the cold water?"

A: "And it wasn't very pleasant!"

Q: "But it was worth it ..."

A: "It sure was! They were so big! I really miss that. There are only a few places where you can get oysters in the river. A lot of the places are closed for oysters."

Q: "When your father was oystering, was this for the family, mainly, or did he sell them?"

A: "No, he didn't sell them at all. He was very fast opening oysters. He opened them for special people that he liked, and relatives. We ate a lot of oysters. We ate 'em fried and raw, scalloped – any way you could fix them. I never got tired of oysters!"

115

Q: "Did you have a favorite way of preparing them?"

A: "No. Not really. Any oyster was good."

Q: "Was there any trick to culling oysters or collecting them? Any tricks of the trade that you learned from him?"

A: "No, not that I learned. I didn't know how to open an oyster. That was smart! I'd have cut off my hand probably. For a long time, they knocked off the flatter end of the oyster. They beat it off with the back of the knife or something, I don't know what they used, and then opened the oyster from that end. Then someone came along and showed them how to open it from the hinge. That was so much quicker because they just put the knife in, turned it and opened it right up."

Q: "What's the most oysters you remember your dad bringing in?"

A: "Probably three bushels, something on that order."

Q: "And he'd get that many in how long? A morning?"

A: "Yeah, maybe a couple of hours. We also went mullet fishing with him. He threw the cast net. He was very good at the cast net. A lot of times he fished with two nets, one that he was throwing and one that he put in the boat to get the fish out of. He sold the mullet. He had a smoke house and they'd smoke the oysters. They smoked turtle meat. I hate to say it, but they smoked sea cow when I was little. Manatees at that time, during the Depression, would feed all of St. Lucie, so everyone was down on the dock to get their roast or their piece of manatee so they'd have something to eat."

Q: "Do you remember that?"

A: "I sure do! I remember when they would have a tub full of manatee meat. It was the way we lived. That's the way it was."

Polly Summerlin Moore still lives in St. Lucie Village.

Curtis Whiticar, standing at far right, with a fishing party after a successful trip. His father, A.A. Whiticar, is kneeling with black dog. (Whiticar Family Collection)

Stuart Shark Attack:
First, It Struck a Sailfish

Mention sailfish and people think of Stuart. For years the city has been known as the Sailfish Capital of the World. Charter boat captain and boat builder Curtis Whiticar escorted countless fishing parties into the Gulf Stream off Stuart's coast during his long career. One trip in particular stands out in his mind. A man he remembers only as Mr. Hart had just hooked a sailfish and was trying to reel it in.

"He was gaining on it, getting it closer to the boat, when all of a sudden the water just broke, busted open, and this giant mako shark came out of the water, straight out almost, with the sailfish in his mouth. The mako is a

117

really beautiful fish, very streamlined. The color is what's so fascinating. They have a glow that looks like a neon light, a bluish neon light. He leaped, it looked like to me, maybe 15 feet out of the water."

Q: "Did he have the sailfish in his jaw?"

A: "Right. When he came down he had already bitten the fish in half. Mr. Hart still had the head of the sailfish on his line. I said, well, bring him on in. We'll unhook it and put it in the fish box. He started pulling it in and I got a hold of the leader wire, just to throw it in the box. After I had the head of the sailfish, and a little bit of his body, coming in with the leader wire, I raised it up out of the water. When I did, the mako shark came leaping up for what was left of the fish!"

Q: "Practically into your boat?"

A: "Practically! Right along side. He even brushed the side of the boat."

Q: "How big do you think the shark was?"

A: "I think he was around 9 or 10 feet long. I threw the head and body, what was left of the body of the sailfish, into the fish box. All of a sudden the shark turned around. Apparently there was blood coming out of the drain hole of the fish box. All of a sudden, he opened his mouth and grabbed hold of the corner stern of the boat. You could hear his teeth grinding on the wood before he let go!"

Q: "Did the shark leave any marks on the boat?"

A: "I had a hatch back in the stern of the boat. I lifted the hatch and looked. It didn't seem to be leaking or anything. However, the next time I hauled the boat out, some of the shark's teeth were still in the corner of the boat. I had a piece of brass about a sixteenth of an inch thick by 2 inches wide, brass molding on the corner of the stern. He had bitten right through the brass molding. How he did it I don't know!'

Q: "Sharp teeth!"

A: "One of his teeth broke off right in that metal!"

SAILFISHING OUT FROM ST. LUCIE INLET, NEAR STUART, FLA.

From "Stuart on the St.Lucie: A Pictorial History," by Sandra Thurlow

Q: "Did you ever go shark fishing intentionally?"

A: "I used to hook one once in a while."

Q: "Not on purpose?"

A: "Not on purpose, no."

Q: "What's the biggest sailfish you ever brought in, or hooked and released?"

A: "Well, I've caught some over 8 feet, just slightly over 8 feet. Atlantic sailfish don't grow much bigger than that."

Q: "Do they jump their height?"

A: "Oh yes, they'll jump their height and more. They also do what we call tail-walking. When you first hook them, sometimes they start speeding away with the line. They're leaping, like a greyhound leap, before they really settle away to do more spectacular jumping. Lots of times, they'll tail walk at first."

Q: "I bet that's a sight to see!"

A: "Yes, it is. All their fight is quite spectacular."

Q: "Sailfish often chase a baitfish…"

A: "Pilchers, we call them. During the early part of the season apparently sailfish would be following them. The pilchers would be in a school. When the sailfish would encounter them they would gather around these pilchers. They would circle around with their sail out. The pilchers would come into a ball. First thing you know, these pilchers would be going around in a circle."

Q: "They were trying to protect themselves?"

A: "Apparently they were, but it's just a phenomenon that happens. After they get in a ball, the sailfish charge them and give their bill a couple of strokes sideways and stun them. When the pilchers started dropping, the sailfish would pick them up in their mouth and eat them."

Curtis Whiticar celebrated his 100th birthday on Feb. 13, 2011.

This sign once greeted travelers crossing the Roosevelt Bridge.(Granfield/Ricou Collection)

Remembering a Pet Pigeon and a Dog Named Molly

*B*efore the St. Lucie County Administration Center was built on 25th Street in Fort Pierce, the area was mostly woods. It was a place where some folks took their freshly captured manatees and sea turtles. Jack Favorite grew up a few blocks away in the 1950s. He remembers the woods as kind of an outdoor slaughtering site.

"I call it a slaughtering house, but it was just string set up to stretch out the sea turtles and sea cows."

Q: "Did you go there with your dad? Is that how you knew about it?"

A: "No. I went over on my bicycle and rode around. You came upon these places everywhere in that area."

Q: "It wasn't really a secret at all?"

A: "No. The game wardens kind of looked the other way, because people were hungry back then and it was a good supply of meat and protein. People would ride the beaches with their beach buggies, jeeps. When they got a turtle or two or a manatee, they would bring 'em out there to dress them out and take the good meat home and leave the carcasses there."

Q: "I guess the birds and other animals had a field day!"

A: "Yeah, the buzzards and crows were in great number in the area all the time and they were fat. I always rode my bike over there. My dog was in a wagon behind me. My pigeon flew overhead. This was just part of our adventure."

Q: "Was that your pet pigeon?"

A:"Yes. My brother was in FFA (Future Farmers of America) and one of his projects was raising pigeons. I picked one for my own and everywhere I went she flew above me."

Q: "How long did you have your pet pigeon?"

A: "Basically, until one of the kids in the neighborhood shot her with a shotgun."

Q: "Oh! Why did they do that?"

A: "Just being kids. Being mean, I don't know. I used to ride my bike to high school. At that time, 25th Street and Virginia Avenue – oh, Virginia wasn't there – but 25th was all dirt. All the roads to Dan McCarty (High School) were dirt. When the state college area was a dump, I saw a mother black panther and two cubs. There were regular animal trails all through the area. I was following one trail and she was on the trail that crossed mine. I heard them coming through the bushes, so I stopped, because I thought it was my brother who I was chasing. She stuck her head into the intersection. I stuck my head into the intersection. When I saw her, I froze. She looked at me for about five minutes and then decided I was safe. She went on her way and led two cubs right across in front of me."

Q: "You didn't get between mama panther and her cubs?"

A: "Heavens no! I'd have been mincemeat."

Q: "You wouldn't be here to talk about it!"

A: "We had a dog named Molly. Over on the Little Jim Bridge, there was a coon that stole everybody's fish. They had tried rifles, they had tried coon dogs, they had tried everything to get rid of this coon and nobody could get him, so one night dad took my Molly over. I cried the whole time, because I knew she was going to be killed. She was a dog, but she was really my sister. I considered her that. The first fish that got stolen, my dad reached down, patted Molly on the head, and said sic him! She went back into the swamp there at the end of Little Jim Bridge. It sounded like a war going on, between the barking and the shrieking. After a while, it got quiet. The mangroves began to rattle and out came the dog. She walked right over Little Jim Bridge, just as proud as she could be, and the coon was never seen again."

Jack Favorite, a retired St. Lucie County firefighter, is an active member of the county's historical society.

Curiosities

Section 4

Underwater filming of "Creature from the Black Lagoon" at Wakulla Springs (Florida Archives)

Ex-Swim Coach Chased
'Creature' in 1950s Horror Film

*D*ick Wells organized Indian River Community College's nationally acclaimed swim program in the 1970s. When he was a student at Florida State University in Tallahassee, he played an underwater role in the 1954 horror flick, "Creature from the Black Lagoon." The tale about a beast in the Amazon was filmed at Wakulla Springs in North Florida. Wells first tried out to portray the creature itself.

"I tried the suit on and it was just too small for me."

Q: "What did you do in the movie?"

A: "I chased the creature. Others would spot the creature from the boat and point to it and I would dive. I carried a gun with me. The gun had a product that was really condensed milk. When I pulled the trigger, a big cloud of milk would come out."

Q: "Was that supposed to be underwater gun powder or something?"

A: "Something like that, yes. They put those movies together in little pieces."

Q: "There was the original 'Creature from the Black Lagoon.' Then there were two sequels?"

A: "'The Creature Walks Among Us' and, I think, 'The Return of the Creature.' They made those movies like comic strips, with little strips of tape and then they put them all together. It was really critical that you did everything you were supposed to do, because they hated to waste film."

Q: "You swam underwater without supplemental oxygen. How long could you hold your breath?"

A: "I don't know exactly how long. Most people can't hold their breath longer than five minutes or so. I wasn't down that long. We had supplemental air handy so we could go over and get if we needed it."

Q: "And you swam the crawl underwater, right? You didn't just do a little dog paddle."

A: "Right. They wanted people to be swimming as if they were on the surface, but underwater."

Q: "Can you be seen in these movies?"

A: "You don't see my face. I was bald and they wanted me to have hair so they penciled it in with a makeup pencil. Then they took carbon paper and rubbed it all over my head to take the shine off. They paid us pretty well, not great, but we did almost anything to satisfy their needs."

Q: "For a struggling college student, especially, I bet it was pretty good money."

A: "I think it was $250."

Q: "Do you have the movies? Do you watch them from time to time?"

A: "We have one of them. They made three movies and I think they pasted them together, so it's kind of hard to distinguish who's underwater."

Q: "Did the creature finally get what was coming to him?"

A: "He did. The creature was subdued. In one movie, he came alive again on shore. That was a low-budget movie, to say the least. The safety people were girls from Weeki Wachee Springs who were underwater swimmers."

Q: "Nothing happened to you, but something happened to one of your buddies underwater ..."

A: "He was not a very accomplished swimmer. The hardest part was coming to the surface with the weight belt on and receiving instructions. Treading water and keeping your head up with the weight belt on is not easy. He looked at me and said through the mask, 'I'm drowning.' I held him up. Another time, I went down without clearing my ears and my mask filled with blood. That wasn't very nice to see. Of course, they didn't show it."

Q: "So they had to reshoot that scene"?

A: "Well, yes. It was just one of those things that can happen if you're a little careless, I guess."

Q: "You survived it all, and made a little bit of extra money."

A: "The biggest thing about it was being there and being in the movie. Of course, the money was important at that time too."

Dick Wells was director of athletics at Indian River Community College, which is now Indian River State College, from 1973-79. He designed and guided construction of the aquatic facility on the main campus in Fort Pierce.

'Creature' pauses to pose during filming of horror flick. (Florida Archives)

Local Builder Once Raised
a Gaggle of Geese

When long-time Fort Pierce builder O.C. (Pete) Peterson was growing up in Wisconsin, his mother treated his sore throats with goose grease. She'd take grease from a Canadian honker, smear it on a sock and wrap the sock around Pete's neck. Much later, after moving to Fort Pierce, Peterson raised some geese of his own. A friend in Tallahassee gave him eight goose eggs and he brought them home in his truck.

"I wrapped the eggs in a towel with hot water, and took them out to Mac Varn's when I got home. Mac was a great raiser of ducks, goose, wild birds. He put them in his incubator and within two days they started hatching, so I hatched seven out of the eight eggs."

Q: "How did they get along without a mother? You became kind of a surrogate."

A: "When I took the little goslings home I had them out in a small little cage and he said do not put water in there where they could try to swim, because they would turn upside down. They have to have their mother's grease on their wings. I'd just put water out and they'd stick their neck through the fence to drink. I had my shop then and I leased part of the 16 acres to Dow Nursery. They had two big irrigation ponds, so when the goslings got big enough I would lock the gates so no one would see me and I would act like Mother Goose. I would go into one of the irrigation ponds and they would follow me and they learned to swim."

Q: "They followed you in a single file?"

A: "In a single file, but they learned to swim, and they grew up to full size, all of them."

Q: "Nobody ever saw you play the role of Mother Goose, Pete?"

A: "No, thank goodness. They would have thought I had gone bonkers! I fed them all the time and they were as happy as they could be, but all of a sudden I missed one. I hunted all over the 16 acres, and couldn't find any wings. They're fighters."

Q: " So if there had been wings that would have meant a predator had fought with them."

A: "That's correct. I had seen fox out there and of course there were coons. There was a panther out there at one time."

Q: "And where are we talking about? How far west of Fort Pierce?"

A: "Jenkins Road, which is just a mile and a half, two miles, from town."

Q: "Anyway, you started missing some of your geese."

A: "Yes. I'd miss one and I'd look all over for feathers. I thought that maybe the predator ran off with it. Then, in a couple of weeks another one was missing. This went on until I didn't have any left. I finally figured out somebody was having goose dinners."

Q: "A human predator, perhaps?"

A: "Yes."

Q: "Goose meat. How does it taste compared to turkey and chicken and duck?"

A: "It's darker. Well, goose and duck, wild ducks, taste about the same."

Q: "You never ate any of these pets, right?"

A: "No. No, heavens no. I couldn't possibly eat one of my little goslings. They had a pecking order, and I called the leader Mother Goose."

Q: "Is that determined by size or just plain old bossiness?"

A: "They're all practically the same size."

Q: "What determines the pecking order? Just who's stronger or pushier?"

A: "Yes, the one that's pushy and most aggressive, that's the leader. You have that even in people."

Q: "So you never used any of the grease from these geese to treat a sore throat?"

A: "No. It was only my mother's remedy. After I left Wisconsin I forgot all about goose grease. I never did appreciate being wrapped with goose grease and old socks."

O.C. (Pete) Peterson has been building homes and commercial buildings in Fort Pierce for more than 60 years.

Seven Gables House Sold for $10 in 1930

*T*he House of Seven Gables, with its breezy porch and storied history, has long been a museum on Indian River Drive in Fort Pierce. It used to be on U.S. 1, and was built as a private dwelling in 1905. By the time John Slay bought it for his large family in 1930, the Great Depression had taken hold. A daughter, Elodie McCready, remembers growing up there. Her brother-in-law, Cookie Eggers, knows the story of how much Slay paid for the house.

"He paid $10 and an old hot water heater, which later injured my wife when she tried to light it one morning."

Q: "Why in the world was he able to get it for such a good price? Cookie, what do you know?"

A: "As far as I can tell, it was hard times, just about what we're having right now. Yeah, it was hard times."

Q: "We're talking about a house that has seven gables and lots of bedrooms but only one bathroom, and that was for a family of nine children and two parents. Mrs. McCready, tell me what it was like. You were one of seven girls in the house."

A: "Well, just like my mother told us, you get in there and do what you have to do and get out. You don't fool around!"

Q: "The bathroom?"

A: "Yes."

Q: "So seven girls had to get ready for school at the same time?"

A: "That's correct, and here's another thing. On chilly mornings my father used to build a fire in the fireplace and we'd all grab our clothes and run in there so we wouldn't be cold while we were getting dressed."

Elodie McCready, who turned 93 in 2010, grew up in this house. (Photo by Janie Gould)

Q: "What were the sleeping arrangements? How many bedrooms?

A: "Actually, we had three bedrooms, but the one bedroom upstairs in the back was very big, so we had two double beds and a single bed in that bedroom. We all had a bed to sleep in. We didn't have to sleep on the floor!

Q: "It was kind of like a dormitory!"

A: "That's what we called it. In fact, we had a line put up back there – our father did that – where we could hang our clothes. Back then we didn't wear slacks and shorts like we do today. We all had dresses or skirts and sweaters, so we had clothes from one end of that room to the other!"

Q: "And your parents had a dry cleaning business, so did the clothes get washed and ironed there?"

A: "Not the clothes that had to be washed, because our mother had a Maytag washing machine. So she washed our underwear and our slips and things. But our good clothes we took to the dry cleaner."

Q: "And you worked there, so you took care of some of your own clothes there."

A: "Oh my goodness, yes! I made sure mine got done, especially if I had a date. I couldn't leave my clothes at home because this one here would put them on and wear them!"

Q: "You're pointing to your sister!"

A: "My sister Lynette, yes. A lot of times, if what I wanted to wear was at home, I'd take it to work with me and then bring it back so I'd be sure I had it!'

Q: "Guarding it from your sister!"

A: "That's right!"

Q: "At that time, the house was on U.S. 1."

135

A: "Of course, it was only two lanes. Right across the street was this little barbecue place, Lewis Barbecue, and then right next to it was this little shop where this lady made all kinds of little trinkets. It was a little gift shop, so any time we were invited to a party, all we had to do was call Mrs. Wagner and tell her we were going to a birthday party or a baby party and she'd have our gift all wrapped for us."

Q: "Did you go downtown on Saturday to the Sunrise Theatre and the shops on Second Street?"

A: "Oh my goodness, yes. Everybody did. Downtown was crowded every Saturday."

Q: "There'd been rumors over the years that the house was haunted. Any evidence of that when you were living there?"

A: "No. I had heard that years ago, but I didn't pay any attention to it. Nothing scared any of us there."

Elodie McCready used to own Chuck's Seafood Restaurant on South Beach in Fort Pierce. She proudly reveals her age as 93, and goes to the House of Seven Gables every Tuesday afternoon to serve as a volunteer tour guide.

Woman holds her nose near a sulphur water fountain in St. Petersburg (Florida Archives)

Sulphur Water: New Floridian Had to Choke it Down

O klahoma was still reeling from the lingering effects of the Dust Bowl when Roy Schick and his family lived there. In 1947, Schick, along with his parents and younger brother, traveled to Florida and visited a relative in Vero Beach.

"This was the promised land! All this greenery. The ocean! Four months later my parents had sold or given away everything they owned and we were living in Vero Beach, where there was a tremendous shortage of housing."

The Schick family was able to rent a small house at the old Naval Air Station at Vero's airport. The Navy base had trained pilots for serving in World War II. After the war, the Navy turned the base over to the city. There were a few houses there.

"My brother and I were the only children out there. We had the run of the naval base. We played in the airplane dump. That was really fun! We took instruments out. We took the control stick out. We did just about anything we felt like doing out there. They had a fire station out there, and the fireman's duty was to watch primarily for brush and woods fires. His name was Gene Ledford, and my brother got to know him. There was a great big fire truck with water cannon. My brother, who was 11, would go over after school and if they had a fire he would ride up on top of the truck with the water cannon. Gene would follow along on the edge of the fire and my brother would put out the fire with the water cannon."

Q: "Truly a volunteer firefighter! You hadn't been in Vero Beach long before you got your first taste of sulphur water..."

A: "Yes. Some people who lived down on the Dixie ..."

Q: "When you say down on the Dixie, what are you talking about?"

A: "Old Dixie Highway! They invited us, I think it was after church, to have dinner with them."

Q: "And when you say dinner, you're talking about noontime..."

A: "Yes. There was no such word as lunch in those days. It was a very nice fried-chicken dinner, but we had ice tea made with sulphur water and I'm telling you I can still remember trying to be polite at the table with my mother glaring at me."

Q: "For people who have never tasted sulphur water, how would you describe it?"

A: "I've heard it described as rotten eggs. If you lived outside the city, you had sulphur water. You had a flow well. There was no electric power or anything. Underground pressure just sent the water to the top. Artesian water, I guess, would be the formal name for it, but everybody just called it sulphur water from the flow well. It was never called artesian water until the yankees started moving to Vero Beach! "

Q: "While you were growing up, you had some odd jobs. You cleaned offices and businesses while you were in high school, and helped at an ice plant when the ice plant was making the transition to refrigeration."

A: "I cleaned Mr. (Joe) Earman Sr.'s offices. He was the major owner of the Citrus Bank. He owned the ice plant and he had ice trucks, but Mr. Earman saw that electric refrigerators were going to be the coming thing and it came fast. One day Mr. Earman decided to rearrange the refrigerators he was selling. He sold Crosleys and something else."

Q: "This was at the ice plant? He sold refrigerators along with ice?"

A: "That's true. One day he asked me to help him move refrigerators. I was a kid of 14 years old. He cautioned me and said, now Roy, be sure not to lift up from the front. That puts all the weight on me! We had no dolly or anything. Mr. Earman and I through sheer force moved the refrigerators around."

Q: "How did the refrigerators sell at first?"

A: "It didn't take long for the ice delivery system to go south, as people bought refrigerators."

The Breakers, a Palm Beach landmark for more than a century.

Palm Beach Boasts a 'Two-Legged Historic Landmark'

Palm Beach's only certified "two-legged historic landmark" was giving a tour recently of The Breakers hotel, which Standard Oil and railroad magnate Henry Flagler built 115 years ago. James Ponce was 93 in 2010. He's a Florida native and member of the oldest documented family in America, the Salanas. His family also has a link to Juan Ponce de Leon, who discovered Florida and the Gulf Stream.

Q: "You're a native of St. Augustine, and your father was the undertaker at Henry Flagler's funeral …"

A: "I'm sure that was the highlight of his career. He always spoke about it with great pride. Flagler wanted to be taken back to St. Augustine and put into the beautiful, beautiful Presbyterian church he built there. He died here in Palm Beach. They say that people waited up through the night for the passing of the Flagler funeral train, all decked out with black like a head of state it was! When it arrived into St. Augustine – they used to have the roundhouse there -- each of the engines blasted their steam whistles one after the other, and my father said he had quite a time holding Nelly, the horse that drove the hearse."

Q: "As the official historian of The Breakers, what's the biggest change you've seen there?"

A: "You know, I think the thing that changed the whole lifestyle you see today was the airplane. Before, people packed a steamer trunk and were perfectly happy to bring their tux and long gowns. My goodness , when I first came to work at this hotel, a man wouldn't even come down to the lobby in the morning without a coat and tie on."

Q: "Was that required at breakfast, even?"

James Ponce gives historic tours of The Breakers
(Photo courtesy of The Breakers)

A: "Oh yes, but you didn't have to tell people. They knew what was expected of them. I remember (The Breakers) finally went from six nights a week in formal attire to Wednesdays and Saturdays and then just Saturdays and now we have a hard time getting a coat and tie on people to go into our gourmet dining room!

Q: "Maybe no cutoffs or tank tops allowed?"

A: "That's pretty hard to enforce, actually, because people feel that they're on a vacation and things should be very casual."

Q: "Who's the most interesting guest you ever saw?"

A: "One of the delights was when Bette Davis was staying here. When she was leaving, they asked if she could leave other than through the front door because there were a lot of people to see her off and ask for autographs and she didn't like that. I met her at the elevator. I'm hoping she'll say something 'very Bette Davis,' you know. I opened the door and she said thank you. When she got out to the top of the steps, she turned to me and said, 'Oh how lovely! Black limousines! I've been station wagoned to death since I've been here.' Pardon my poor imitation!'

Q: "If the walls of The Breakers could talk, what's the most interesting story they might tell?"

A: "Oh, I don't know what that would be. I remember once I was giving a tour and someone said, well, this late in the season I guess there aren't any celebrities here. I said, well, when we turned the corner, you'd almost think that was ex-President Nixon talking to Chet Huntley. Well, that was ex-President Nixon talking to Chet Huntley."

Q: "You were named Palm Beach's only "two-legged historic landmark."

A: "That's right. When they got up to number 200 of the markers that go on the houses, the mayor and town council decided to do something special with it. They awarded it to me as a two-legged landmark and came over here to The Breakers to present it to me. I took one look at it and said that's the biggest damn tie tack I ever saw!"

James Ponce, who is retired as assistant manager of The Breakers, has been giving historic tours of the property for nearly 30 years.

Kerosene, Raw Bacon Served as Home Remedies

*W*hen most Floridians lived far from doctors, kerosene was often the best medicine. Audrey Hopson of Palm City, Joyce Crouch of Fort Pierce and Wilford Underhill of Okeechobee grew up with 10 other siblings on a farm along the Kissimmee River. They say kerosene practically worked miracles.

"For a bad cold, before you got pneumonia you would take a teaspoon full of sugar and put coal oil or kerosene on it," Underhill said. "You would eat that and that would break up the inflammation in the lungs. The reason you used sugar, kerosene would have done the same thing, but if you got strangled on the kerosene it would kill you. So you put it on sugar. That way, you would eat it and wouldn't get strangled on the kerosene."

"And when we would get a cut on our foot, Mama would get the kerosene and she would pour it on that and it would heal it," Hopson said.

"And also," Underhill said, "if the kids would step in hot ashes – we'd always have a camp fire -- kids would step in hot ashes and burn their feet or whatnot, or if you got burns from the stove, you take motor oil. Daddy would pour it in a pan. If it was a kid's feet they would put their feet in that motor oil and it would draw every bit of the heat out."

Q: "Did it happen to you?"

A: "Oh yes. It happened to me, and I distinctly remember it happening to a niece."

Q: "And did it work?"

A: "Oh yes. It worked. And then another thing: This happened to me and it happened to my youngest daughter. She got a fish hook in her foot. Of course, we took the fish hook out and that night it got infected and started swelling and she couldn't sleep for the throbbing. We took a piece of bread, put two pieces of bacon on it, a copper penny, and tied it to that foot. In a little while that baby went to sleep, and when we pulled that off we could see the corruption, where it had driven the corruption out of there. It healed up and there was no more problem."

Q: "Cooked bacon?"

A: "No. just regular old raw bacon, white bacon, and a copper penny on the bread. I guess the penny was to hold it and the bread was to absorb the corruption that it pulled out, because, I mean, if you leave it on too long it'll draw so much that it'll start hurting."

Q: "So there was no way to get a tetanus shot but that did the job?"

A: "That did the job. For a fish hook or a nail or anything that would cause an infection that would be the trick."

Q: "Where did your mother learn that?"

145

A: "I have no idea. It was just one of those old things that was handed down from the old-timers on down."

Q: "Did you ever see a doctor when you were growing up, any of you?"

A: "Yes, we did," Hopson said. "Before any of us here were born, mama had typhoid fever when DeWilton was a baby and almost died. After that, every year daddy would take us to the doctor in Frostproof and we had to have a shot. That's the only time I remember going to the doctor."

Q: "The rest of the time home remedies did the job?"

A: "You always had kerosene because your lamps and some of the heaters and stoves ran off it," Crouch said.

Q: "Electricity didn't come to your farm until when?"

A:"I went into the Navy in 1950," Underhill said. "Along about then we got electricity and they ran a telephone line in."

Wilford Underhill, Audrey Hopson and Joyce Crouch are among seven surviving children of William Freeman and Mary Underhill. The parents were born between Frostproof and Fort Meade in 1888 and 1893, respectively.

The Vero Drive-In stood near the present site of Outback Steak House on U.S. 1.
(Provided by Jack & Sara Chesnutt)

Baby Chick Giveaway Caused U.S. 1 Traffic Jam

*T*he drive-in theater was a postwar icon. Parents would pack up their Baby Boom kids and everyone enjoyed an evening of inexpensive entertainment. Jack Chesnutt opened the Vero Drive-In in 1950.

"Admission then was 44 cents, and children under 12 got in free. Of that 44 cents the theatre only got 37 cents because there was still an excise tax from World War II: 20 percent."

Q: "What were the prices of the food?"

A: "Oh, it was terrible. Hot dogs were 15 cents and the drinks! I think the regular size was 10 cents and the large was 15. We did have lots of mosquitoes. I got DDT spray from Mosquito Control. We had 55- gallon drums on the back of a truck and it went through the exhausts. We sprayed for mosquitoes and it really made a difference."

Q: "You were telling me about a promotion you did around Easter."

A: "This was probably the second year we were open, and I came up with the idea. I talked to Law's Feed and Supply, and they agreed to give us 3,000 baby chicks to give away. Actually, we didn't give them away. We gave certificates. Anyhow, we advertised 3,000 baby chicks to be given away on that Easter Sunday, and would you believe the cars were lined up from the drive-in theatre all the way into town! Some people even brought containers to put the chickens in, but we gave them certificates to go to Law's and pick up 15 chicks. U.S. 1 was totally bogged up. They had the police there trying to direct traffic and everything. We filled up and still had cars that couldn't get in!"

Q: "Lots of chicken dinners over the next few months?"

A: "I guess so. It was a different lifestyle from what we have now."

Q: "You did this on Easter Sunday in conjunction with the movie that was playing?"

A: "I don't remember the name of the movie that day. It was just a promotion. The chicks kind of go with Easter. New birth."

Q: "I guess a lot of people in town had chicken coops."

A: "Well, actually, when I moved to Vero Beach in 1933, we lived in a house right across from where city hall is. We had our own chicken yard and we had chicken every Sunday. I was the one who had to kill the chicken and pick it. My mother took it after that."

Q: "So that type of thing was still going on, especially when practically everyone in town got 15 baby chicks!"

A: "You can't even raise chickens in the city of Vero Beach now. It has changed."

Q: "You were showing me a picture of a teepee that you had outside the drive-in. Chief Crazy Hoss. That's H-O-S-S. What was that all about?"

A: "Universal Films came out with a Drive-In Theatre Week. They offered prizes for the best exploitation of their movies. The one that I chose to do was Chief Crazy Horse. Ted Morris had a Model-A Ford, and we built a teepee on it and drove it all around town. I submitted that and won as the best exploited picture in the United States that week. I was awarded all of $250."

Q:"It helped drum up business?"

A: "Well, in the theatre business it's called exploitation. I don't think the theatres do that much anymore, but we used to do it a lot. You're always trying to come up with something different – gimmicks. I remember one time at the Florida Theatre we put a house on the back of a truck and drove around town advertising a movie. I can't even remember the name of that one."

Chesnutt also managed the indoor Florida Theatre. At the drive-in, teens sometimes slipped in without paying by hiding in the trunk of a car. "Pretty soon after we opened, we had ramp boys. After the show had started, one of 'em went and leaned up against a post watching the movie. The car he was next to had a couple of kids in the trunk and they couldn't get out. They were in there about an hour. Maybe they learned a lesson."

Q: "I was going to get to that and ask if you ever checked trunks when people were coming in."

A: "No, we did not. Some of the kids came in from behind. We knew that and we didn't worry about it. They would buy stuff at the snack bar."

Q: "As long as they did that, it was OK?"

A: "That's right."

The screen tower at the drive-in was built in triangular design to withstand hurricane winds.

"And it did, but it didn't withstand the wrecking ball later!"

The Vero Drive-In, which was near the present site of the Outback Steak House, was closed in 1980. The Florida Theatre on 14th Avenue was closed a few years later.

Marquee announces the closing of the drive-in in 1980.
(Provided by Jack & Sara Chesnutt)

Slot machines confiscated in Daytona Beach photo (Florida Archives)

Slot Machines Used to be Nearly Everywhere

One-armed bandits were part of the South Florida landscape during the Great Depression. Slot machines, legal and otherwise, "sounded their merry clatter in drug stores, filling stations, emporiums and even fish camps" during the 1930s and 40s, as a newspaper put it. Frank Pearce of Vero Beach is a retired optometrist and highly decorated veteran of World War II. He worked in a drug store in Miami while he was going to high school.

"In those days the slot machines were everywhere in Miami."

Q: "So that type of gambling was legal in those days?"

A: "It's hard to say if it was legal or not. It was widespread. No one was being prosecuted for it."

Q: "So it was overlooked? Winked at, maybe?"

A: "Overlooked."

Q: "Were children allowed to use the slot machines, or was it adults only?"

A: "It was adults only."

Q: "How much money could somebody make?"

A: "It would probably be $100 or $150."

Q: "And the machines took quarters and even dimes?"

A: "Yes, and if three bars came up you had a winner."

Q: "I guess you heard some yelling and screaming sometimes."

A: "Oh yes."

Frank Pearce was acquainted with a family who were heirs to a milk fortune. The elderly matriarch used to frequent the drug store where he worked, and not just to get her prescriptions filled.

"She would come down and play the slot machines when she was too old and didn't have the strength to pull the lever. So she would give me a quarter to stand by and pull the lever for her. I never saw her win any huge amount but she had a great time."

Q: "How long did the slot machines last?"

A: "Pretty much while I was growing up, until World War II came along. Then everything changed, in many different areas."

Q: "And the slot machines vanished?"

A: "Vanished."

Q: "You were telling me there was a club in the middle of Biscayne Bay, a gambling club of some sort."

A: "It was called the Bikini Club. Pretty wild, with whiskey and gambling and slot machines. But it was rigged so that if the law enforcement people came along, they could pull a lever and a false door on the barge would open and the machines would fall into Biscayne Bay."

Q: "How did you hear about that?"

A: "I went by there one time, on a boat."

Q: "When was the Bikini Club around?"

A: "It was after the war."

Q: "But those were the only slot machines that were in evidence at that time. Right?"

A: "Right. The Mafia was pretty much in control of a lot of that."

Q: "They controlled the slot machines in the drug stores?"

A: "Yes, they did."

Q: "Did you ever see a Mafiosa?"

A: "Not to my knowledge."

Q: "What's your most treasured memory of your childhood in Miami?"

A: "My friends in the neighborhood. In those days kids weren't sitting in front of computers. They made their own forts and tree houses. In those days you weren't frowned on for riding your bike to school. I rode my bike to high school. Today it would be uncool."

Q: "And there was a lot of vacant land, even in Miami, at that time."

A: "On North Kendall Drive there was vacant land as far as you could see!"

Frank Pearce completed 25 combat missions in Europe as a B-17 bomber pilot during World War II. He worked as an optometrist in Coral Gables for 35 years and retired to Vero Beach. He died July 17, 2011, at the age of 87.

Waldo Sexton poses with members of the Dolphinettes, a synchronized swim team, at Sexton's Mountain in about 1960. (Sexton Family Collection).

Only Remnant of Sexton's Mountain: Memories

O nce there was a mountain in Vero Beach. Sexton's Mountain was an oddity that rose on the barrier island across from Jaycee Park. The eccentric entrepreneur Waldo Sexton had finagled some fill dirt from a man who was dredging the river. A grandson, Sean Sexton, says Waldo got much more he bargained for.

Workers build steps at Sexton's Mountain in this undated photo from the late 1950s. (Sexton Family Collection)

"I think the guy had already figured Waldo out. He put the pedal to the metal on that dredge and he filled up that lot with river bottom that stacked up higher than the trees around it."

Q: "Waldo never expected to see a huge mound of dirt?"

A: "I've heard that he was surprised. The pile sat there, because he didn't have that many low places to put it in. This is when it became a mountain in his mind, so he began to put the accoutrements of the mountain on it. It started out as a rustic kind of thing, with big slabs of concrete that were put in place as steps. Over time he began hauling things to the mountain site: pedestals from an old water tower, Corinthian columns, certainly tiles. He had mounds of tiles in his dairy pastures that he used to decorate the steps of his mountain. He called the stairs the Santa Scala, the Holy Stairs."

Q: "I remember at the top there were two thrones. They looked like they might have been those of Aztec gods. Where did they come from?"

A: "Entirely out of his imagination! They were things that were fabricated from things that he had. I still use things from Waldo's goody piles all the time."

Q: "You have a blueprint here that shows he was going to call it the Hanging Gardens of Vero."

A: "It was going to be the centerpiece of an artists colony, Ponce de Leon Park. He about figured that Ponce de Leon must have landed right about there. It's funny. I've read a National Geographic article that actually puts (the landing) somewhere between Melbourne Beach and the (Sebastian) Inlet."

Q: "So Sexton's Mountain was going to be an artists colony!"

A: "He had a lifelong obsession with the arts, and he wanted to be an artist. I think that the mountain was maybe a final expression of that desire. Beanie Backus told me he tried so hard to teach Waldo how to paint and it just absolutely couldn't be done. But Waldo was, as we understand the creative spirit, very much an artist."

157

Q: "You were a young boy when the mountain was dedicated. Do you remember it?"

A: "I remember when my sisters and I went over to climb the stairs. We were taken to the opening of the mountain. It was always there along the highway, A-1-A, and people were always stopping in to climb, but once the stairs were finished there was this grand event. It just seemed like it was the highest thing in the world."

Q: "Does anybody know exactly how high above sea level it was?"

A: "A geodetic survey was performed and it found it to be the highest point between Kitty Hawk and Key West. There have been many claims about its actual height."

Sexton Mountain lost its luster over the years, because vandals chipped away at the tiles and marred them with graffiti. By the time Waldo Sexton died in 1967, any talk of an artists colony was long forgotten. But the big pile of dirt remained until 1984, when a Nor'easter blew into the beach. Two Sexton properties, the Ocean Grill and Driftwood Inn, were nearly washed into the ocean. Workers managed to save them by shoring them up with dirt from Sexton's Mountain.

"The mountain wound up in the place where all mountains go – the sea. I guess it all turned out the way it was supposed to. There are a lot of things of which the only thing remaining is the story."

Sean Sexton is a cattleman, artist and published poet, and he's the author of an illustrated book about Sexton's Mountain.

About the Author

Janie Gould, a fourth-generation Floridian who lives in Vero Beach, earned a bachelor's degree in journalism at the University of Florida and worked as a writer and editor for newspapers and magazines for more than 20 years. She started the WQCS oral history project in 2005 and has been interviewing people for radio features ever since. She created the award-winning Floridays show in 2008. Her radio interviews are also heard every week on Florida Frontiers, a half-hour newsmagazine produced by the Florida Historical Society. The show is aired on public radio stations throughout Florida. She has been honored for her work by the historical society and the Associated Press.

She is a member of the board of directors of Vero Heritage, Inc., the Indian River County chapter of Children's Home Society, and the Pelican Island chapter of the Theodore Roosevelt Association. She is a former president of the Indian River County Historical Society and a former board member of the Florida Historical Society.

She also is a member of Vero Beach Opera, Inc. and its piano scholarship committee. She is a classically trained pianist who is a student of Dr. Marcos Daniel Flores, and is the pianist at Trinity Episcopal Church in Vero Beach.

Made in the USA
Charleston, SC
17 October 2011